NURSING HOME MINISTRY

A
MANUAL

TOM & PENNY
McCORMICK

Ministry Resources Library

Zondervan Publishing House • Grand Rapids, MI

Nursing Home Ministry: A Manual
Copyright © 1982 by Frank C. Horton.
Zondervan edition published 1987 by special arrangement with
Great Commission Publications, Philadelphia, Pennsylvania.

Ministry Resources Library is an imprint of Zondervan Publishing House,
1415 Lake Drive, S.E., Grand Rapids, Michigan 49506.

Library of Congress Cataloging in Publication Data

McCormick, Tom.
    Nursing home ministry.

    Bibliography.
    1. Church work with nursing home patients—Handbooks,
manuals, etc.   I. McCormick, Penny.   II. Title.
BV4435.5.M37   1987   259'.4   87–6219

ISBN 0-310-34571-5

Quotations from the following are used by permission:

The *New American Standard Bible*. Copyright © 1971, The Lockman
Foundation, La Habra, Calif.

The *New English Bible*. © the Delegates of the Oxford University Press and
the Syndics of the Cambridge University Press 1961, 1970.

Edited by Michael G. Smith

Printed in the United States of America

87 88 89 90 91 92 93 / CH / 10 9 8 7 6 5 4 3 2 1

FOREWORD

This manual for ministry in nursing homes was itself born and nurtured in ministry. Its editor, Tom McCormick, has been uniquely well qualified to compile it and to contribute to it. He has been engaged in many important activities; his name has become synonymous to those who know him with ministry to residents in nursing homes. Although he is young, he has long had a love and a constructive concern for the institutionalized elderly. For some years he has conducted services in nursing homes and has personally ministered to numerous nursing home residents. He is well acquainted with the inner working of a nursing home and as an employee of one home has learned how to work effectively with members of the staff. He has consulted and prayed with people who share his concerns, has read the pertinent literature and above all has sought to set forth and follow thoroughly biblical principles.

Tom has for several years given instruction about nursing home ministries in a segment of a course in practical theology at Westminster Theological Seminary. He has also served as coordinator of such ministries in the Philadelphia area under the sponsorship of New Life Presbyterian Church. In this capacity he helped organize churches and individuals in an attempt to supply a ministry of the word of God to all the nursing homes in the Philadelphia area that were open to it. As he engaged in this effort, he became persuaded of the need to provide instruction for Christians in nursing home ministries. He consequently began to conduct seminars in churches and to plan and develop this manual. After much prayer, study, reflection and consultation, a first edition was issued in mimeographed form with the request that readers send in suggestions for its improvement. Now that a considerable period of testing has passed and a thorough revision has been made by Tom and his wife, Penny, the manual is being officially published.

Your prayer is solicited that this handbook, which has been born and nurtured in ministry and prayer, will assist in bringing forth extensive and intensive ministries in nursing homes in many places. And prayer is in order that one special fruit of its ministry will be that the residents or older people who are ministered to in the way that it recommends will themselves be stimulated to minister to others and to reach out in their prayers to the whole world.

The Skilton House   John H. Skilton

77014

TABLE OF CONTENTS

PREFACE

This manual for working with the institutionalized elderly (the "Nursing Home Manual" as we have always called it) had its beginning in the basement of Skilton House, a center for Christian ministry in Philadelphia. John Skilton had long been visiting in several nursing homes in the area. Tom moved into the House to help in the ministry, and gradually others joined John in his vision to have a Christian witness in every nursing home in Philadelphia. It soon became obvious that some kind of instruction was needed to help newcomers to the ministry and to encourage and enlarge the scope of activity of those already involved. Thus the manual was born—not a theoretical ideal, but a practical response to pleas for help.

The manual is intended primarily for use by Christians who wish to carry on a Christian ministry. We have not tried to hide the fact that our beliefs pervade every area of our lives. We maintain that everything we do should be firmly rooted and grounded in Scripture. Not that the manual is for use only by a spiritual elite. Clergy and laymen, new Christians and those more experienced should all benefit from this book.

Our purpose in writing the manual is threefold. First, to help those who are seeking to start a ministry with the elderly, but don't know where to begin. For them the manual offers some tried and tested suggestions for taking those first steps. Second, we aim to encourage those already involved and give insight as to how they could deepen their ministry through enriching their understanding of older people, involving others and so on. Third, the manual is written to challenge those who have forgotten or are not aware of the needs of the elderly. It presents a biblical mandate to which we all should respond with changed attitudes and actions.

The manual is designed to be used in varied ways. Some may wish to read it cover-to-cover. Others may choose to look up specific topics of interest or material on particular needs and questions that have arisen in their ministry. The manual can be used equally well for personal study or for small groups such as Sunday school or church home meetings. Some have found it helpful in sermon preparation, others have consulted it as a resource in conducting seminars on ministering to the elderly. From its inception the manual has been designed *to be used*. It is our prayer that it will not be an ornament on a shelf but will continue to encourage, stimulate and challenge its owners through its continual use.

To thank everyone who has been a part of the creation of the manual is impossible. There have been so many who have selflessly offered time and expertise in its various stages of production. A few, however, deserve special mention and thanks: John Skilton for his vision, prayers, thoughts and gracious example; Georgina Dietz, Greg Donovan, Wayne Mack and Judith Shelly for their help on the early stages, particularly with regard to biblical material; all those who attended the first brainstorming potlucks at Marlene Hammerschmidt's (special thanks to Marlene); Jim Petty and Church of the City (in Philadelphia) for their invaluable counsel and support over many years; Dr. George Fuller for providing the opportunity to share and refine this material at Westminster Theological Seminary; Sharon Fish for her insights and editing from the perspective of a nurse, writer and longtime laborer with older people and for her contributions to the bibliography; Tom Church for his encouragement, example and contributions to the bibliography; Betsy Allinson for her copy editing and advice; Page Allinson for his fine photography skills; Roberta Morton for her many hours typing the final manuscript.

There are many who no doubt deserve mention whose names do not appear here. These are those who volunteered their resources—counsel, typing, writing, editing, words of encouragement, exhortations—in the first years of the manual's history. Without those first working copies of the manual, this present edition would not be available today. So to each bearer of even a cup of cold water we say, you shall not lose your reward (see Matthew 10:42).

Above all we thank those older people who have loved us, taught us, put up with our mistakes and encouraged us with their enthusiastic appreciation of whatever we had to offer.

We would like to hear from you. Please write to us if you are interested in receiving a newsletter on nursing home ministries. It will deal with special topics of interest, models for ministry and requests for prayer and will keep us in touch with what others are doing. We would appreciate your insights and suggestions.

Write to: Nursing Home Ministries
Skilton House
930 Olney Ave.
Philadelphia, Pa. 19141

We also want to thank Tenth Presbyterian Church in Philadelphia, New Life Presbyterian Church in Jenkintown, Pa., and the Committee on Diaconal Ministry of the Orthodox Presbyterian Church for their financial support in the production of the manual.

Tom and Penny McCormick

PART I

ORIENTATION

If someone is going to consider taking part in a ministry to the elderly, he needs to know what is required. He must come to grips with the needs. He must discern what the word of God directs him to do. He must assess his own gifts and recognize his strengths and weaknesses. And, above all, he must develop a genuine concern for the welfare of those to whom he would minister.

Part I has been put together to help such a person orient himself to the tasks and challenges of a nursing home ministry. Read and ponder the sections you find there before you begin to wrestle with the how-to in the subsequent parts of the manual.

PLEASE RESPOND

by Calvin Freeman, Geneva College

Anyone who visits nursing homes has stories to tell, and I am no exception. The stories point to the tremendous need.

Mr. Joseph Dean was a lonely man. He was living at the Geriatric Center and there were few people there with whom he could communicate. He was deeply interested in spiritual things; he liked to talk about the Bible and problems related to it. Mr. Dean had no living relatives that I know of, and only occasionally did any friend have time to visit him—so he was very much alone. Mr. Dean longed for release from the pain and anguish of his world.

"I was disappointed when I woke up this morning," he told me one day.

"Why?" I asked.

"I prayed last night that when I awoke this morning I would be in heaven. Instead, when I opened my eyes I found I was still here!"

Mr. Dean's experience was not all that unusual. The number of happy people in a nursing home often is quite small.

It is difficult for someone to lose not only his friends, but also his independence. Mr. Dean was confined to bed and was totally dependent upon the nursing assistants who might not be able to come when he needed them. There were times when he sat for hours on a bed pan waiting for the nurses to come.

I remember well one lady with Parkinson's disease who was unable to keep her hands from jerking and who, though she enjoyed reading, was finding it more and more impossible. This lady, who gave no evidence of being a Christian, would ask, "Why me? Why is this happening to me?" I remember another elderly lady from a Christian Science background who was in great pain as she lay dying with cancer. I remember telling her of the nature of Christ—that he was not just man but both God and man. "To think," she repeated over and over again, "I have been wrong all these years." She thanked me for telling her and at that time gave evidence of committing herself to Christ, the eternal Son of God.

Another lady, who had been a nurse and had spent her life sacrificing and giving to others, told me that she had always expected that when she became old there would be someone to do the same thing for her that she had done for others. It was a big disappointment for her to learn that her own life of giving was not a guarantee that she would be remembered when she was old. Her own daughter, married to a millionaire, did not have time to bring her postage stamps.

These examples point to some of the many needs that exist among the aged. But it is not enough merely to become aware of the needs. We must also become aware of our obligation as Christians. I think of the passage in James which tells us that faith without works is dead. The Christian simply cannot face needs without at the same time becoming aware of the obligation.

> If a brother or sister be naked, and destitute of daily food, and one of you say unto them, Depart in peace, be ye warmed and filled; notwithstanding ye give them not those things which are needful to the body; what doth it profit? Even so faith, if it hath not works, is dead, being alone.
>
> James 2:15–17 (KJV)

I think also of that well-known passage from St. Paul's letter written to the church at Philippi. God's people are called upon to have in them the same mind which was in Christ Jesus. We are not to be preoccupied with ourselves but rather we should be deeply concerned about the needs of others, even as Christ was willing to forget his own rights to the privileges of heaven and in obedience to his Father humiliate himself on this earth, making himself of no reputation and becoming obedient unto death, even the death on the cross (see Phil. 2:4ff.). These two passages point to the obligation that is placed upon all Christians to forget themselves and to follow their Lord by showing mercy and love for those who are in need. This lifestyle of service after the manner of Christ is filled with countless blessings and innumerable rewards. Please respond.

HONOR

Wherever we turn in the Bible, we consistently see exhortations to honor the aged. In the Ten Commandments (Ex. 20:1-17) we find the well-known commandments to honor father and mother, whatever their age. Other commandments prohibit afflicting or taking advantage of the widow (for example, Ex. 22:22). Leviticus 19:32 also makes our attitude to the elderly abundantly clear: "You shall rise up before the grayheaded, and honor the aged . . ." The New Testament likewise promotes an attitude of honor as it reiterates the command to honor parents in particular (Matt. 15:1-9; Eph. 6:2, 3) and the elderly in general (1 Tim. 5:1-3).

The scriptural examples of honor and dishonor give us a clearer idea of exactly what honor is. In relation to honoring God through sacrifice and through his Son (Mal. 1:6-14; 1 Sam. 2:27-30; John 5:22, 23) we see that to honor is to esteem, revere, regard, respect, give recognition to, or recognize the value, importance, or significance of someone. Some antonyms and divergent concepts are to despise, reject, mock, show contempt for, be ashamed of, or speak evil of someone (Is. 53:3; Ps. 22:6, 7; Deut. 28:49, 50; Prov. 30:17).

Honor is an attitude of the heart which issues in action. In Matthew 15:1-9 Christ condemns the attitude of the Pharisee who says that he has pledged his belongings to God so he doesn't have to give them to his needy parents. Christ describes this action as putting the traditions of men (pledging to God) before the commandment of God (honoring parents).

Assuming that we do have a heart attitude of honor, how can we make it complete by showing honor through our actions? The Bible has some helpful suggestions. In the Old Testament we see God's care for the widow as he protects her (Ps. 68:5—physical, psychological needs), provides for her (Deut. 14:28, 29—material needs), includes her in feasts (Deut. 16:10-15 —social, cultural, spiritual needs), shows special compassion on her (Ex. 22:22; cf. Is. 9:17—emotional needs), and executes justice for her (Deut. 10:18—legal needs). In the New Testament, honor involves taking care of, giving priority to (Matt. 15:1-9; Rom. 12:10-21). First Timothy 5:1-8, 16 tells us how to provide for the needs of widows. John 19:25-27 shows us—as a model—Jesus' care of his mother.

With these examples in mind it is not hard to see many ways in which we can honor the elderly in nursing homes. Good manners such as rising when they enter, not calling them by their first names until they ask us to do so, knocking on their doors before entering, asking permission to enter or sit down—these are obvious ways to show honor. In addition, we can honor them by listening well—to their sorrows, their reminiscences, even their complaints.

Note: Part III of this manual ("Visitation") gives many helpful and workable suggestions that can be implemented as you visit elderly folk in your own local nursing homes.

When honoring the elderly seems especially difficult, remember that in God's view of things the greatest honor is given to what is often considered the least honorable (1 Cor. 12:12–26). It is a privilege and a blessing to stand firm against the ways the world views things and to see with the eyes of God as we honor the elderly.

MINISTRY TO THE ELDERLY:
AN OUTLINE FOR BIBLE STUDY

This outline should help you discover, if you don't already know, what Scripture has to say concerning the elderly, their role in the family of God and the responsibility the church has to minister to them.

The purpose of the outline is to get you in touch with the relevant passages of Scripture. The next stage depends on you. Plan to spend some time in the passages that are listed below. Get yourself a notebook to record your reflections and insights as you study.

Don't try to work through the whole outline in one sitting. There is too much there. Instead, work through only a portion of the outline at one sitting, in keeping with a plan and schedule that will take you through the whole within a week or so.

Tag these passages in your Bible. You will find yourself wanting to share many of them with people you will be meeting in your ministry.

I. A biblical view of the elderly and aging

    A. Old age can be a privilege.
        1. Old age is a blessing.
          a. It is a sign of the blessing of the Messianic Age.
            (1) Is. 65:20 (see vss. 17–25). With reference to the new heavens and the new earth long life is assured.
            (2) Zech. 8:3–5; Jer. 31:13. When Jerusalem is restored, the old will be there.
          b. It is a reward for piety.
            (1) Deut. 30:19, 20. Loving obedience to God is rewarded with long life.
            (2) Ex. 20:12. Honor to father and mother results in long life.
            (3) Job 42:16, 17. Job's perseverance was rewarded with long life.
            (4) For further study, Ps. 91:14–16; Eph. 6:1–3.
          c. It is a token of divine favor.
            (1) Gen. 15:13–15. Abraham is assured of God's blessing of old age.
            (2) Ps. 128:5, 6. To live to see one's grandchildren is a blessing of God.
            (3) 1 Sam. 2:31, 32. Lack of age implies a curse.
          d. Old age, however, is not always a blessing.
            (1) Deut. 28:50. God curses those who do not obey him; this curse bears on the elderly.
            (2) Is. 3:5; 9:14, 15; Jer. 51:22b. God is no respecter of

persons in his chastisement and punishment. The details of these curses are of interest.
2. Old age is honored and respected.
   a. Honor of old age in the Old Testament.
      (1) Lev. 19:32. "You shall rise up before the grayheaded, and honor the aged, and you shall revere your God; I am the Lord." Our attitude of honor manifests itself in behavior.
      (2) For further study, see Job 29:8; Wisd. of Sol. 2:10; Ecclus. 8:6.
   b. Honor of old age in the New Testament.
      (1) 1 Tim. 5:1, 2. The old are to be treated with the same honor due to our parents.
      (2) 1 Pet. 5:5. The younger are to be subject to the elder.
      (3) For further study on the honor due parents, see Ex. 20:12; Lev. 19:3; Deut. 5:16; Eph. 6:1–3; Matt. 15:1–9; Mark 7:6–12.
   c. The honor of the old is recognized as a new kind of beauty (cf. Prov. 20:29; 16:31).
3. God's covenant promises are given to the elderly.
   a. Is. 46:3, 4. God's faithfulness is constant, being manifested as compassionate care to his elderly saints.
   b. Ps. 71. Here a righteous man prays to God in his old age, praising him for his righteousness and faithfulness (vss. 19, 22–24), and calling upon God in his time of need. The whole psalm deserves careful attention.
   c. Ps. 103:5. God renews the youth of his people (cf. Is. 40:28–31).
   d. John 3:4–8. God can give new life even to the elderly.
   e. Ps. 92:14, 15. God promises fruitfulness to the elderly.
   f. Ps. 146:5–9; 147:3, 6; Jas. 1:27. Widows are a privileged class for God's care and provide a model for our care of the elderly.
      (1) Ps. 68:5. God protects the widow.
      (2) Deut. 10:18; 27:19; Is. 47:6. God executes justice for the widow and curses those who pervert justice for the widow.
      (3) Deut. 14:29; 26:12, 13; 24:19–21; Acts 6:1–7; 1 Tim. 5:1–16; John 19:26, 27. God provides for the financial and material needs of the widows.
      (4) Deut. 16:10, 11, 13, 14; Zech. 8:3, 4. God makes special provisions to include the widow in the covenant life of his people. Here they are to rejoice at the feasts of God *with* his people. This may well indeed have implications for the presence of the elderly at the Lord's Supper, the New Testament feast of God.
      (5) Is. 9:17. God's special attitude toward the widow is

compassion.

   (6) 1 Tim. 5:1–16. Further New Testament applications are detailed here.

   (7) Luke 7:11–17. Jesus has compassion on the widow of Nain, exercising his redemptive power on her behalf.

B. Old age can be a time of special trial.
  1. Old age can be a time of fear and anxiety.
   a. Ps. 71:9–13ff. The vulnerability and weakness of old age is a special concern even for the righteous.
   b. Eccles. 12:1–7. This is often read as a classic description of the infirmities of old age. The Good News Bible provides an especially helpful translation.
  2. Old age can be a time of failing health.
   a. Eccles. 12:1–7. This description is worth a rereading.
   b. Gen. 27:1; 48:10; 1 Sam. 4:15; 2 Sam. 19:35; 1 Kings 14:4. The eyesight and senses of the elderly often fail. (For a positive benefit of this, see 2 Cor. 4:16–18; 5:7.)
   c. 2 Cor. 4:16–5:10; 1 King 15:23. Age brings decay to the outer man.
  3. Old age does not always diminish strength.
   a. Deut. 34:7. Moses was strong and healthy at 120 years of age.
   b. Josh. 14:10–12. Caleb also remained strong into his eighty-fifth year and was ready for further adventures.

II. The opportunities and responsibilities of the elderly

A. God's expectations of elderly Christians.
  1. Old age provides opportunities.
   a. Ps. 71:18; 48:13. Old age provides an opportunity to show God's faithfulness.
   b. Ps. 90:12; Heb. 5:14. Old age provides an opportunity to become wise.
   c. Lev. 19:32; Rev. 1:14 (Dan. 7:13). Old age provides an opportunity to "picture" God, the Ancient of Days.
   d. Matt. 24:13. Old age provide an opportunity to persevere.
  2. The elderly can be a benefit to others.
   a. Job 12:12; I Kings 12:6 ff. The wisdom gained through long life can benefit others.
   b. Ps. 37:25. The experience of the elderly can provide spiritual encouragement.
   c. Ezra 3:10–12. The elderly can be a source of tradition, order, "roots."
  3. Elderly saints are presented to us in Scripture in several ways.
   a. Ps. 92:12–15. Here the righteous elderly are pictured as a flourishing tree.

(1) Vs. 12. The elderly are to flourish and grow in faith (cf. Ps. 1:1–3; Phil. 1:9; 1 Thess. 4:1).
(2) Vs. 13. The elderly are to be in the house of the Lord (cf. Eph. 2:19ff.; 1 Pet. 2:4–10, esp. vs. 5; Heb. 3:6).
(3) Vs. 14. The elderly are to bear fruit (cf. John 15; Gal. 5:22, 23; Matt. 5–7; Eph. 4–6; 2 Cor. 4, 5). Inner character development is always a responsibility and opportunity for the Christian.
(4) Vs. 15. The elderly are to display and proclaim the Lord's uprightness, steadfastness (cf. Ps. 71:15, 24; 37:25; Phil. 1:19–26).

b. Luke 2:25–38. Simeon and Anna are two New Testament illustrations of Ps. 92:12–15. Notice as many specific correlations as possible between these two saints and the picture in Ps. 92.

c. 1 Tim. 5:5, 6. Here the "real widow" gives us a picture of what is expected of the elderly Christian woman. These then are expectations and responsibilities that may be held up to both young and old as goals (see vss. 9, 10 for the bearing of these goals on the "pre-widows").

d. Titus 2:2–5, 11–15. Paul gives specific commands to the old men and the old women. Notice the authority with which these instructions are commended in verse 12.

e. Eccles. 11:8; Joel 2:28; Acts 2:17; Zech. 8:4 may be consulted for further study.

B. Responsibilities of the non-Christian elderly.
1. Everyone is under obligation to love God with all his heart, soul, mind and strength, and his neighbor as himself.
2. "All have sinned" (Rom. 3:23) and are called to repent of their sin and believe in Jesus, the Lamb of God who takes away the sin of the world.
3. All men, then, must submit to the lordship of Christ Jesus (Phil. 2:10).

III. The church's responsibility toward the elderly

A. The church's responsibility to the elderly begins with Christians (Gal. 6:10).
1. Lev. 19:32; 1 Tim. 5:1, 2 (see I, A, 2 above). The church must honor the elderly.
2. Jas. 1:27; Matt. 25:36. The church must visit the elderly.
3. Ps. 71:9, 18. The church must not forsake or cast off the elderly.
a. Deut. 16:11, 14. The elderly, especially the widows, are to be included in the community life of the church. Do not accept the pattern of isolation of the elderly so often imposed

by the world around us.
    b. 2 Sam. 19:31-40. The desire of the elderly to stay at home should be honored.
    c. 1 Tim. 5:4, 8, 16. The family has a special role to play in the care of the elderly. The church has a responsibility to teach families to be obedient to God's word at this point.
    d. 1 Tim. 5:3, 9ff.; Deut. 14:29. The church is called upon to provide for certain widows.
  4. Ps. 68:5; Deut. 10:18; Ex. 22:21-24; Jer. 7:6. Even as God executes justice and protects widows, the church as the body of Christ surely must be like God in this concern.
  5. The church's responsibility to the elderly includes preparation for old age—and that starts early—and the prevention of future difficulties.
    a. Ps. 71:6; John 15:1-11. The elderly need to be taught to trust God. This starts from childhood.
    b. 2 Tim. 1:5; Gen. 17:7; Ruth 4:14-17; John 19:26, 27. Covenantal families must be developed.
    c. 1 Tim. 5:10-16; Titus 2:2-5, 11-15. The elderly must learn what is expected of them.
    d. Titus 2:3-5. Opportunities for the elderly to instruct the younger are vital.
    e. Gal. 6:7ff. The aging process needs to be understood: there are physical, mental and spiritual consequences of our manner of living.
    f. Ps. 1:2. Here development of a life of prayer and meditation is encouraged.

B. The church also has a responsibility to non-Christians.
  1. Gal. 6:10. We are to do good to all men as we have the opportunity.
  2. Matt. 28:19, 20. We have been commissioned by our Lord to make disciples of all nations. Certainly we are not to overlook the elderly in our desire to proclaim the gospel of eternal life to all men. The love of God is to be expressed in word and deed.

IV. Ministering to the elderly

A. The motives for working with the elderly.
  1. 1 Cor. 10:31. To bring glory to God.
  2. 2 Cor. 1:3-7. To worship and thank God.
  3. Gal. 5:6. To show our faith.
  4. Matt. 7:24-27; Matt. 25:31-46; Jas. 1:22-25; 1 Tim. 5:1-6. To obey God's commands.
  5. 1 Cor. 12:12-27; Rom. 12; Col. 2:19; Eph. 4:15, 16. To build up the church.

B. The privilege of working with the elderly.
    1. Matt. 25:40; Rom. 8:29; 2 Cor. 3:18. To be with Christ in his work, becoming more and more like Jesus.
    2. Gal. 2:20; 1 Tim. 3:13; Jas. 1:25. To know more of God's love, mercy and compassion through Christ in us ministering to others.
    3. 2 Cor. 4:18. To be involved in the temporal sickness and suffering that so often point up the eternal realities: life, death and judgment.
    4. Is. 65; Zech. 8:4, 5; Rev. 21, 22.

C. Suggestions for working with the elderly.
    1. Show deep care for their needs—physical (encourage the staff, pray for needs); emotional (visit, listen, pray); and spiritual (conduct worship services, read Scripture, pray).
    2. Encourage the development of talents and abilities of the elderly.
    3. Encourage friends outside the nursing home to join you in your efforts.
    4. Be sensitive to family and community relations that the elderly have. Encourage these others to become more involved.
    5. Give small gifts or cards on birthdays and/or Christmas, etc.
    6. Share the greatest gift of all—salvation through Jesus Christ.

As you look through the rest of this manual, you will read more about many of these suggestions, about how to make these goals more concrete. Don't be overwhelmed by the number of suggestions. Start with one area where you think God is calling you to work—and move on from there. We have made relatively few suggestions, really. We trust God will bring others to your mind, so that the ministry to the elderly may be as varied and rich as possible.

QUALIFICATIONS FOR BEING A SERVANT OF CHRIST

God wants to use us to serve him and bring him glory. Although he has created each of us as a distinct individual, there are certain qualities that we should have or be striving for if we are to minister to others. Reflect on the following Scripture passages and assess your qualifications for service to Christ.

For God so loved the world . . .   *John 3:16*

God loved us enough to give up his only Son to die for our sins. Knowing and experiencing that love is crucial as we carry on a ministry to the elderly. Without continually being sustained by God's abiding love, without drawing deeply from the wells of salvation, there is no strength, no life, no joy in our ministry. "We love, because He first loved us" (1 John 4:19).

"My sheep hear My voice, and I know them, and they follow Me."
John 10:27

The Bible is very clear about what it means to hear and follow Jesus. Matthew 25:31–46 gives some practical ways to follow—feeding the hungry, showing hospitality to strangers, giving clothes to the poor, visiting the sick and the prisoner. Are you willing to be not only a hearer of the word, but a doer of it also (Jas. 1:22)? If you aren't, says James, then you delude yourself.

We know love by this, that He laid down His life for us; and we
ought to lay down our lives for the brethren.
1 John 3:16

One quality we should expect to see in a servant of Christ is a sacrificial love like his. Philippians 2 tells us that Christ gave up his heavenly home and became a servant, obeying God even to the point of death. This should be our standard of love—not merely words, but self-giving deeds (see 1 John 3:18).

But if we are afflicted, it is for your comfort and salvation; or if we
are comforted, it is for your comfort . . .
2 Cor. 1:6a

The Christian life is characterized by affliction—affliction that comes from knowing Christ, "and the power of His resurrection and the fellowship of His sufferings, being conformed to His death" (Phil. 3:10). These afflictions may not require martyrdom, but they may involve sickness, loneliness, financial insecurity, rejection by friends, grief, or any number of the things that Christ suffered and in which we join him. The comfort we receive from knowing that God's hand is on our life equips us to minister comfort and salvation to others. Is your response to affliction like that of Paul who said, "Blessed be the God and Father of our Lord Jesus Christ, the Father of mercies and God of all comfort" (2 Cor. 1:3)? Don't be bitter about suffering: let it prepare you to comfort others.

What are some practical ways in which we can show our love for God and for others as faithful servants of our Lord Jesus Christ? One way is by simply being a good listener. Sometimes people just need to share their burdens and hopes and cares with another person. Be ready to respond with a sympathetic or encouraging word. Your role as a servant requires that you accept people as they are—it's okay to be weary, confused, weak, even angry. Ask yourself what you can do to help their situation. Remember: we are commanded to bear one another's burdens (Gal. 6:2).

Another way to show your love to the elderly is by being committed to regular visitation. This may be difficult at times, but if your motives are sincere, then a sacrificial attitude will be easier to maintain. Nurses have mentioned the negative effects of sporadic visitation, which increases depression and behavioral disorders. Consistent visitation, however, shows that we are true friends who deeply care about the individual.

A cheerful face is always encouraging for the elderly person—but remember to "weep with those who weep" (Rom. 12:15). In a humble spirit, be prepared to share your faith in Christ at an appropriate time.

If this seems like a lot for one person, remember that you don't have to be perfect! Trust in God to overcome insufficiencies and mistakes—then go ahead and enjoy making new friends.

VOLUNTEERS NEEDED FOR MINISTRY IN NURSING HOMES

1. *Listeners:* For visitation ministries these volunteers are the most important. Almost anyone qualifies for this task. Suggest this role especially to those who think they are ungifted or useless.

2. *Musicians:* Individuals, groups, vocalists, instrumentalists, the young (e.g., youth choirs), the old—all can be used in special programs or in worship services. Don't neglect recruiting song leaders who can help teach songs and lead nursing home residents in both familiar and new songs.

3. *Miscellaneous Performers:* They can be used in a talent show or special performance. Don't overlook any talents: storytelling, singing, dancing, poetry reading, joke telling and instrument playing (see "Conducting a Variety Show" in the appendix for some recommendations).

4. *Travelers and Naturalists:* Travelogues and nature presentations in the form of movies or slides are good since they provide visual interest to accompany the personal oral presentation.

5. *Artists and Crafts Specialists:* Use such people either to teach or to make a presentation/display of their specialties.

6. *Recreation and Tour Leaders:* Keep alert to activities that are suitable and not too taxing for elderly persons who are able to enjoy and participate. Church suppers and picnics provide opportunities for such volunteers.

7. *General Helpers:* These people can be used for bringing the elderly to worship services, helping them find hymns, leading in singing, or just giving moral support to others. Such volunteers are greatly appreciated and always needed.

8. *Preachers and Teachers:* Both the ordained and unordained are helpful for worship services and Bible studies.

INITIATING A NURSING HOME MINISTRY

Beginning a ministry to the elderly in nursing homes may seem an overwhelming task to plan and implement. But it is precisely good planning that will help make your ministry happen.

Evaluate your resources—they are of prime importance in planning the type and scope of your ministry. Who will help you in this activity? How much time do you have? What gifts and interests do you and others have? All these factors will determine what type of ministry you can have (worship service, adopt-a-grandparent, room-to-room visitation, variety show, etc.), its frequency (weekly, bimonthly, monthly), and its magnitude (five people, one floor, a whole nursing home). As you evaluate your resources it is imperative to assess your commitment and motives as well.

Begin to gain an understanding of elderly people. Reading this manual is one way to start. Continue your reading among many helpful books listed in the bibliography. Perhaps you and others could visit several nursing homes in your area as an informal way of becoming acquainted with the situation of the elderly.

Assess the needs of the particular home you wish to visit. Naturally you will understand these needs much better as you become more involved. Begin by discovering what kinds of programs they already have and the general physical condition, morale and spiritual health of the residents.

Choose a program that is appropriate to the needs of the home, as well as to your own resources, interests and commitment. Pray that God will guide you in this important decision. Be prepared to adjust your plans as you gain a deeper understanding of the home and the individual elderly with whom you come in contact there.

Make an initial contact with the nursing home either by phone or in person. If there is an activities director, he would be someone to talk to in addition to the director. Explain who you are, whom you represent and what goals you have. Be as specific as you can be about your plans. How you word things is important. Some nursing home administrators may understand "evangelism" to mean "proselytizing."

If they are willing for you to begin a program there, establish a time and place to begin. If possible, also arrange a meeting with the chief administrators: the director of nursing, the activities director and the director/administrator. You want to be sure to know all the responsible people in the home and to be known by them. Give them a clear and concise presentation of your goals, activities, etc. Make sure they know what church you represent, your pastor's name, and the primary contact person they should call with their questions or suggestions.

As time progresses you will have an accepted (and—hopefully—valued) place in the life of the home. Consequently, you will have more freedom. Be prepared to go slowly and wait for the freedom to be given to you, rather than demanding too much too soon.

LOOK CLOSER AND SEE THE REAL ME

(Found in a geriatric ward of a hospital in Scotland — author unknown)

What do you see, tell me, what do you see?
Who are you seeing when you look at me?
A crabby old woman, not very wise,
Uncertain of habit, with far away eyes
Who seems not to notice the things that you do,
And forever is losing a stocking or shoe.
Is that what you're thinking? Is that what you see?
Then open your eyes, for you're not seeing me.

I'll say who I am as I sit here so still,
As I rise at your bidding and eat at your will.
I'm a small child of 10 with a father and mother,
Sisters and brothers who love one another.
A young girl of 16 with wings on her feet,
Dreaming that soon her true sweetheart she'll meet.
A bride at just 20, my heart gives a leap,
Remembering the vows I promised to keep.
At 25, now I have babes of my own
Who need me to build a secure happy home.
A woman of 30, my children grow fast,
Bound to each other with ties that will last.
At 40, my grown-up sons will be gone,
But my man stays beside me to see I don't mourn.
At 50, once more babies play round my knee,
Again we know children, my loved one and me.
Dark days are upon me, my husband is dead,
I look at the future, I shudder with dread.
My children are busy with babes of their own,
I think of the years and the love I have known.

I'm an old woman now, grace and vigor depart,
But thousands of memories live in my heart.
Inside it, you see, a girl still dwells,
And now and again my tired heart swells.
I remember the joy, I think of the pain,
And I'm loving and living life over again.
So open your eyes, please open and see.
Not a crabby old woman, look closer—see me!

PART II

NEEDS

The thrust of a Christian ministry to residents of nursing homes is a response to the personal needs that the elderly have at this time and place in their lives. In this part of the manual you will become better able to identify some of the common needs and concerns and better prepared to respond to them.

The first section has been written to help you identify and understand some of the typical needs and concerns that one finds among the elderly. In the chart that follows the descriptions, each need/concern is listed and related to other needs/concerns. The chart shows what biblical passages are relevant for the need/concern and suggests a proper way of approaching and responding to it. The purpose of the chart is not to give the final word on each need/concern but to get you thinking about it and preparing yourself to respond to it.

IDENTIFYING NEEDS AND CONCERNS

Read through the short description of each need/concern below. Then, in order to put each one into focus and begin thinking about how to respond to it, consult the same need/concern on the chart that follows.

Anxiety

Casting all your anxiety upon Him, because He cares for you.   *1 Pet. 5:7*

There are many potential causes of anxiety. What may seem trivial to one person can be a crisis to another. Remember this as you visit the elderly. Their worries may be in a totally different realm from yours, but that is no reason to dismiss their problems, or fail to understand how they feel. Listen as they explain their worries about finances, death, whether or not they will walk again, the future—whatever it may be. Try to feel with them.

We who are believers have a God who loves and cares for us more deeply than our friends, relatives or nurses can ever care for us. There is really no reason to worry about *anything* if we are trusting in God and loving him. The unbeliever, however, has everything to worry about. To such a person you must point out that in spite of the good care he may be receiving from people he must trust Christ in order to have no worries. Do your best to find the root cause of the anxiety, and wherever possible help to change the circumstances that create the anxieties.

Comfort

"Blessed are those who mourn, for they shall be comforted."   *Matt. 5:4*

While you yourself are not the ultimate source, you can be one of the greatest means of ministering comfort to the elderly. Whatever the cause of distress—death of a loved one, loneliness, fear—your consistent visitation and sympathy will be much appreciated. Let them lean on you but beware if they begin to develop an unhealthy attachment to you as their only source of comfort. A comfort that does not have its source in the unchanging and merciful God is only a temporary and unstable comfort. The comfort you are able to give is the comfort you have received (2 Cor. 1:3–11).

Contentment

. . . I have learned to be content in whatever circumstances I am.   *Phil. 4:11*

Much lack of contentment stems from fear and an excessive concern for one's self. Thus the major effort of the visitor should be to displace this concern. If the person to whom you are ministering is merely distracted for a while by your presence, then the problem will not be solved. You must help him find another focus for his attention, a focus that will give lasting satisfaction. The only such focus is God. This is not to say, however, that there are not many practical things to be done. For example, if the person needs a friend, *your* friendship can be a great source of contentment.

Death

"O death, where is your victory? O death, where is your sting?"   *1 Cor. 15:55*

The best way to prepare for death is to be so overwhelmingly involved with Jesus that you can hardly wait to meet him face to face! You can help the elderly develop such a relationship in several ways: Make it a priority in *your* life to have such a close relationship with Christ. Share as clearly and as often as possible what Christ means to you. Comfort the elderly as they experience the death of friends and relatives. Use these occasions as opportunities to talk to them about their own death. Be aware of the grief that will invariably come with the dying process (cf. "Grief" below). And, finally, take time to deal with your own attitudes about death and share openly with them about your struggles in this area.

Economic Adjustment

. . . I count all things to be loss in view of the surpassing value of knowing Christ Jesus my Lord, for whom I have suffered the loss of all things, and count them but rubbish in order that I may gain Christ.   *Phil. 3:8*

You can help to ease the pain of those who are in financial and material need.

First, *do* something about the need — organize a clothing drive in your church, share what you can of your resources, solicit donations (for a pair of special shoes, for example). But be careful not to overwhelm your friends with charity so that you destroy their proper sense of self-worth. Second, stress the relative unimportance of material things in comparison with eternal things. We know a dear Christian who, on an allowance of four dollars a week, is constantly trying to give money away to us! Contentment with your physical state is possible when you know God is caring for your needs.

Fear

"Do not be afraid, little flock, for your Father has chosen gladly to give you the kingdom."   Luke 12:32

The first and most important thing to do is to find the basis of any fear. Whether it is real or imaginary, it needs to be dealt with. Then begin to help your elderly friend to focus his mind on new thoughts and concerns (see "Thought Life" below). Be careful not to take his mind off the fear too quickly. If the fear has not been "exorcised," it will likely return.

Grief

. . . that you may not grieve, as do the rest who have no hope.   1 Thess. 4:13

It is helpful to see grief as occurring in three stages (see *The Christian Counselor's New Testament,* Jay Adams, 1977, pp. 730, 731). The first stage, or *crisis* stage, is characterized by surprise, shock and emotional release. This is the time to lend a listening ear. The second, or *crucial* stage, is one of disorganization. Ties to the past must be broken, and the future viewed realistically. The person may be feeling a whole range of emotions—fear, anger, guilt—and will need help in sorting through what has happened. The *construction* stage is a time for creating new patterns of living which are not tied to the past. A friend can be helpful in setting new objectives, especially a friend who can help make Christ the center of the new life.

Hope

. . . Christ in you, the hope of glory.   Col. 1:27

It is important to hear what a person is saying is the cause of his despair. Christ is indeed the answer to all our needs, but his name should not be lightly offered as a blanket remedy for all ills—especially those that we know nothing about because we haven't listened! Only after we know the problem can we *apply* Christ's hope to a specific situation.

Loneliness

Do not cast me off in the time of old age; do not forsake me when my strength fails.   Ps. 71:9

Encourage the person to be outgoing in making friends with both staff and residents of the nursing home. He can start with a smile, a kind word and a cheerful attitude—and work from there. He is not alone in his loneliness, and befriending others is one of the easiest ways to make friends. For those who are bedridden, encourage others in the home to visit them—even take a visitor with you when you visit! Remember, too, that *you* are a friend—don't visit sporadically, but give of yourself and your time to be a friend.

The Past

. . . forgetting what lies behind and reaching forward to what lies ahead, I press on toward the goal for the prize of the upward call of God in Christ Jesus.   Phil. 3:13, 14

Don't assume that all dwelling in the past is wrong. Perhaps there is anger, bitterness or guilt that needs to be discussed. Don't press too hard if the elderly aren't willing to talk about a problem; they are sometimes more reticent to discuss openly than we might be. Do urge taking these matters to God in prayer and if possible clearing things up with the people involved. Give them things to do and think about in the present, too. Involvement with other people and their needs is a good way to become freed from too much introspection. Remember, too, that often the past is worthy of much enjoyable reflection and reconsideration.

Peace

"Peace I leave with you; My peace I give to you; not as the world gives, do I give to you. Let not your heart be troubled, nor let it be fearful."   *John 14:27*

As with contentment, God is really the only source of a lasting change, since he alone can give true peace. As you minister to older persons, stress what the individual can do about his relationships to others that will bring peace. There may be a need to forgive others, for example, or to deal with bitterness from the past. Encourage them to be examples of peace and so receive the gift of peace.

Physical Decay

Therefore we do not lose heart, but though our outer man is decaying, yet our inner man is being renewed day by day.   *2 Cor. 4:16*

Gradual decay of the body is to be expected. Don't be repelled by the aging bodies you see—look to the unseen, the spiritual, the persons beneath the sometimes feeble bodies. Let them know you still care—especially by a loving touch of that body they may have come to dislike. Point them to the unseen too—encourage a close, personal relationship with Christ. This will help them to become more excited about the prospects of an eternal life with Christ—one in which there is no pain or death. Encourage a reliance on God as a source of strength—physical and otherwise—*now.*

Self-Esteem

See how great a love the Father has bestowed upon us, that we should be called children of God; and such we are . . .   *1 John 3:1*

It is most important that we focus on God's grace and power in our lives as the source of our self-esteem. Others will come to appreciate this if we give testimony to it in our selves. Encourage those to whom you are ministering to come to God in humility and accept his love for them *as they are.* As a visitor you are a great source of self-esteem as you show love and concern for individuals no matter what their physical, mental or spiritual state. There are, of course, various personality-building exercises that can build self-esteem—things that require stopping sinful practices (such as complaining and gossiping) and living a life of love. The external things should not, however, take the place of the need for a changed heart.

Thought Life

Set your mind on the things above, not on the things that are on earth.   *Col. 3:2*

Where our desires and thoughts are focused is where we live. Our thoughts are crucial in how happy and fulfilled we are. The same is true for the elderly. If we deal only with outward behavior, then there will be no true change or healing. God and his attributes must be the center of thought and action.

Time

Making the most of your time, because the days are evil.
                   Eph. 5:16

The need for discipline in the use of time is crucial for the elderly who no longer have their former obligations, responsibilities and patterns of life. As a consequence, many older persons in nursing homes spend much of each day gazing at a television set or off into space. There are usually some activities in which the residents can be involved—craft programs, therapy, social events. As enjoyable and valuable as these activities are, they often lack the deep sense of meaning and purpose that the human heart craves. We all need to see that our time is not our own, and the elderly are no exception: time is a gift from God which is to be used to its fullest to his glory. Brainstorm with friends as to what the elderly can do that is meaningful and enjoyable, then approach the nursing home with suggestions. Everything—including prayer, knitting baby booties or visiting others in the home—counts.

NEEDS AND CONCERNS CHART

How to Use the Chart

For Personal Preparation

The chart that follows was composed in response to a need to deal specifically with problems encountered by individuals we have known in various nursing homes. The chart also has proved useful in the preparation of sermons for use in the homes. In connection with each major need/concern we have listed a number of related areas of concern so that you can be aware of the many varieties of needs and concerns that exist. We have offered scriptural references to help you ponder and address the many needs/concerns listed. We are convinced that one important way to understand the thoughts and feelings of the elderly is to spend time meditating on God's word.

Under each need/concern there are three columns of information:

Related Concerns

These are areas of concern related to the main topic of the chart. Since people respond to situations in different ways, we have tried to touch on some of this variety and to suggest both problems and solutions that you should be aware of.

Bible Study Materials

The passages listed in this section demonstrate sometimes positive and sometimes negative reactions; they may show man's response or God's response. They relate to the need/concern in a variety of ways and are to be used only as a springboard for further meditation and deliberation. In many cases the Scripture passage will be something you can share with a resident. It may be one of the most important gifts you can take with you as you visit. But be prepared to explain it and put it in a context.

Response

Here we offer some suggestions on what to say and do in response to certain needs of the elderly. We have tried to avoid pat answers, but have not always been successful: some pat answers are the truth! Don't be restricted by our suggestions. While the truth to be communicated remains the same, each individual needs a response tailor-made to suit his own specific problem. Be creative!

For Direct Sharing with the Elderly

Sharing Materials

These hymns and Scripture passages are especially suitable for sharing. Consider writing out a hymn or a few verses in large, bold print and leaving it with the person for his own personal meditation. This section of the chart can also be used to suggest ideas for hymns and Scriptures for worship services.

ANXIETY

RELATED CONCERNS	BIBLE STUDY MATERIALS	RESPONSE
Oppression by others	Ps. 42:9	There are two kinds of anxiety-producing situations—those we have no control over and those we do control. Determine which cause is relevant in each situation. If there is something that can be done, help the person do it. Whether it is relieving someone of the task of letter writing or exhorting him to flee from sin, chances are you can bear the burden without becoming anxious yourself.
Unbelief	Rom. 11:19–23; Heb. 3, 4	
Depression	Ps. 42:5, 11; 1 Tim. 5	
Self-indulgence	Rom. 6, 8; Eph. 2:3; 1 Tim. 5:6	
Unfamiliar, unknown surroundings	Heb. 11:8–10	
Disorder of life	1 Tim. 5:11–13	
Too many burdens	Is. 53:4	Listen, console, encourage, act when possible.
Sin	Ps. 38:18	
Sexual frustration	Col. 3:1–6	
God overcomes anxiety	Pss. 16, 46; Is. 41:10; Jer. 17:7, 8; Matt. 6:25–34; Phil. 4:6, 7; 1 Tim. 5:5; 1 Pet. 5:6, 7	Encourage a closer walk with God. He is the only one who can calm the anxious heart because he is the only one who really knows how to care for us. Read Scripture, pray and worship God together. This takes the focus off self and puts it on the good and powerful God. Be alert for especially anxious times such as impending surgery, room changes, etc.

SHARING MATERIALS

Scripture: Pss. 16, 46; Prov. 1:33; Is. 41:10; Matt. 6:25–34; Phil. 4:6, 7; 1 Pet. 5:6, 7
Hymns: Be Still, My Soul/What a Friend . . ./Jesus, Lover of My Soul

See also charts on Fear, Peace; and those that deal with potential causes of anxiety such as Death, Companionship, Economic Adjustment.

COMFORT

RELATED CONCERNS	BIBLE STUDY MATERIALS	RESPONSE
Expressing sorrow	Pss. 6, 13, 88, 102	Study the biblical way of expressing sorrow and grief. Emotions are not meant to be bottled up inside, or to be made known in bitterness, complaining and false accusation. Rather, the elderly should be encouraged to pour out their souls to God.
The comfort of God	Ps. 103:13; Is. 51:12; 55:6, 7; Lam. 3:19–24; Matt. 5:4; John 14:18; 2 Cor. 1:3–5	If God has indeed forsaken us and left us comfortless, then we have reason to remain forever in our grief and sorrow. Remembering what God has done in the past is a good way for Christians to be encouraged that God is faithfully loving us in the present, in spite of how things may appear.
The comfort of Christ	1 Thess. 2:16, 17; Heb. 2:17, 18; 1 Pet. 2:21	Christ suffered and was tempted to sin just as we are. Praise him for the comfort of the salvation we have as a result of his suffering and perfect life.
The comfort of God's word	Ps. 119:50–52, 76	Meditating on God's promises and love for us is a great comfort.
The comfort of others	Gen. 24:67; 2 Cor. 7; 1 Thess. 4:18	God wants us to receive comfort from people as well as from him directly. You can be a bearer of comfort as you share how God has comforted you, as you listen patiently while people pour out their hearts, and as you read Scripture and pray.

SHARING MATERIALS

Scripture: Ps. 23; Lam. 3:19–24; 2 Cor. 1:3–5; 1 Thess. 2:16, 17
Hymns: Leaning on the Everlasting Arms/How Sweet the Name of Jesus Sounds
          Jesus, Lover of My Soul/The King of Love My Shepherd Is

See also charts on Grief, Anxiety, Hope.

COMPANIONSHIP

RELATED CONCERNS	BIBLE STUDY MATERIALS	RESPONSE
The need for companionship	Gen. 2:18–25; John 14:16–18; 1 Cor. 12	We were created for fellowship. We need not be ashamed of loneliness, but neither should we complain or be bitter if God has not given us friends at any particular time.
The purpose for companionship	Rom. 12; 1 Cor. 12; Eph. 4, 5; Col. 3; 1 Tim. 5	Friends should build one another up. Encourage the elderly to say kind words to one another, to encourage the staff, to praise God with other Christians.
Causes of loneliness	Ps. 88:6; 102; Prov. 12:18; 16:18, 28; 17:9, 13, 14, 18–20; 18:1; Rom. 5:3–5; Phil. 1:29; Heb. 12:14, 15; Jas. 1:1–12	If we don't have friends, it may be that our character needs to be conformed more closely to that of Christ. Is there anger, bitterness, a quarrelsome or complaining spirit that makes an individual not the kind of person people want as a friend? Help him deal with this problem. Or perhaps others are sinning by standing aloof from someone who is sick or mentally unbalanced. Show them by example as well as word how to love unselfishly.
Characteristics of a friend	Ps. 35:13, 14; Prov. 17:17; 18:24; 27:6, 10; Matt. 5:43–48; 7:1–6; 18:15–20; Luke 10:30–37; John 15:13; Rom. 12:9–21;14; 15:1–7; 1 Cor. 13; Eph. 4; Heb. 10:23–25	Work on practical ways of showing friendship—a kind word, a small gift, shared food, help with a phone call. There are many ways the elderly can befriend one another.
God as Friend	John 14:23; 15:14, 15; Eph. 2:12, 13ff.; Phil. 4:19; Pss. 90, 91	Show God's love by being a friend yourself. Visit regularly, bring gifts, telephone, write letters, especially on special days like a birthday, Christmas, Valentine Day and Mother's Day. Point to God as the real Friend who will never leave nor forsake, and whom we long to be with forever.

SHARING MATERIALS

Scripture: Psalms; Proverbs; Rom. 12:9-21; 1 Cor. 13
Hymns: What a Friend We Have in Jesus/Jesus! What a Friend for Sinners/God Will
Take Care of You/Leaning on the Everlasting Arms

See also charts on Grief, Self-Esteem, Peace.

CONTENTMENT

RELATED CONCERNS	BIBLE STUDY MATERIALS	RESPONSE
Assurance	John 10:10; Col. 2:2, 3; Heb. 6:10–12; 10:22, 35, 36; 1 John 3:18–22	We have God's promise that if we persevere in doing his will, we will be saved. This is not to encourage salvation by works, but to point to the graciousness of God.
Happiness	Ps. 16:11; 32:11; 36:8; 132:15; Acts 14:17	Knowing who you are (Christ's precious possession) and where you are going (heaven) can give the deepest happiness of all.
Friendship and God's presence	Deut. 30:15; Ps. 16:11; 17:15; 25:14; 65:4b; 90:14; John 15:12–17; Heb. 12:1–3	Evaluate your resources as a friend. What can a person do to make himself a friend to others? Encourage the elderly to get to know Jesus better as their Friend.
Provision for need; and prosperity	Deut. 30:3, 5, 9; Ps. 1; 24:1; 25:12, 13; 37:11; Matt. 5:5, 6; 6:24–34; John 6:35; Acts 14:17; 1 Cor. 3:21–23; Phil. 4:6–12; 1 Tim. 6:5–10, 17–19; Jas. 5:1ff.	We may have a false idea of what our needs are, and think we need what we don't. At times we may suffer lack, but this unites us to Christ as we turn to him in these times of need.
Future	Ps. 16; Eph. 1:18; Col. 1:12; Heb. 1:2; Jas. 2:5; 1 Pet. 1; Rev. 21:4	Discuss the future realistically— if possible, talk about attitudes to death. A personal relationship to Christ makes the future bright rather than dismal.

SHARING MATERIALS

Scripture: Ps. 145:14–16; Phil. 3:7–11; 1 Tim. 6:6–8
Hymns: Blessed Assurance/God Will Take Care of You/I Know Whom I Have Believed

See also charts on Peace, Economic Adjustment, Anxiety.

DEATH

RELATED CONCERNS	BIBLE STUDY MATERIALS	RESPONSE
Death itself	Gen. 2:16, 17; Deut. 30:15–20; 1 Cor. 15; 2 Cor. 4, 5; Phil. 1:20–26; 3:1–11; 1 Thess. 4:13–5:11 (See Westminster Confession.)	If you are ready to meet God, then the main obstacle to ridding yourself of fear is gone. Encourage a living, vibrant relationship with Christ—then there will be more eagerness.
Judgment	Ps. 96:10–13; John 3:4–21; 5:19–30; Acts 17:30ff.; Rom. 2; 2 Cor. 5; 1 Pet. 4:17–19	Explain what judgment is, and how we can avoid condemnation by believing in Christ and committing our life to him.
Suffering, sickness	Is. 53; Rom. 5:3–5; Jas. 5:10, 11, 13–16; 1 Pet.	Suffering, disease, weakness, decay—these are all results of the fall of man. But God is in control of all things—he has not forsaken the sufferer. For the believer, it is a blessing to suffer as Christ suffered. As you offer the hope that we have, don't do it glibly—try to understand objections that may arise, and don't forget to lend a sympathetic ear.
Decay	1 Cor. 15:49ff.; 2 Cor. 4, 5	
Weakness	Ps. 71:9; 2 Cor. 12:9, 10; Phil. 4:13; Heb. 11:34; 4:15, 16	
Models of attitude toward death	Luke 23:46; Acts 7:54–60; Phil. 1:20, 21; Jas. 5:10, 11	By thinking of how others have reacted to death and suffering, we prepare ourselves for our own death.

SHARING MATERIALS

Scripture: Ps. 46; 96:10–13; Is. 41:10; 1 Thess. 4:13–18
Hymns: When the Roll Is Called up Yonder/The Solid Rock/The Strife Is O'er

See also charts on Grief, Fear, Thought Life, Hope and other related topics.

ECONOMIC ADJUSTMENT

RELATED CONCERNS	BIBLE STUDY MATERIALS	RESPONSE
Lack of funds	Matt. 6:26–34; 2 Cor. 8, 9; Phil. 4:10–14; 1 Tim. 5:1–16	Consider how to obey 1 Timothy 5:1–16. Encourage diligence in prayer on the part of the older person (and yourself!). But remember 1 John 3:16, 17.
Poor understanding of money	Matt. 5–7; Luke 6, 12 (cf. 1 Cor. 3:21, 22)	Share from your own life your understanding of the value of material things, and perhaps any struggles you may be having as you seek to conform your life to God's way.
Greed	Eph. 4:17–19; Col. 3:1–6ff.	Teach, rebuke, exhort, encourage.
Robbery	Deut. 28; Ps. 27; 28; 35:9ff.; Heb. 10:32–39	Comfort them in their loss. Consider possible legal action, and see what agencies are available for help.
True hope and true riches	Ps. 16; 1 Cor. 3:21, 22; Gal. 4	Clarify and affirm what is of real value—friendship, love, inner attitudes expressed in life and the eternal relationship with God.

SHARING MATERIALS

Scripture: Ps. 16; Matt. 5–7; Phil. 4:10–14; Col. 3:1–4
Hymns: Count Your Blessings/God Will Take Care of You/He Is All I Need/Thou Art Worthy

See also charts on Fear, Self-Esteem, Contentment, Thought Life.

FEAR

RELATED CONCERNS	BIBLE STUDY MATERIALS	RESPONSE
Death	Matt. 10:28–32; 1 Cor. 15; Heb. 2:14, 15	We need not fear death, because Christ has gone before us to take the sting from death and to make death an entrance into life.
Judgment	Ps. 96:11–13; Rom. 5:1; 8:1; Heb. 10:26–31; 1 Pet. 4:12–19; 1 John 4:17–19	Judgment Day holds fear only for those who have not put their faith in Christ. Stress the need to trust in *his* righteousness, not our own.
The unknown	Matt. 6:31–34; John 14:1ff.; Heb. 11:8–10; 13:5, 6	Worrying about the future will not change it. God is with us, so there is no need to fear what is to come.
Repetition of the past	Rom. 6:4–14, 19–23; Phil. 3:13, 14; 1 Pet. 4:1–3	Discuss the specific situation in the past that is a cause for fear. Find ways to learn from mistakes. Pray for release from repetition of the past, and trust God that he will answer.
Illness and suffering	Ps. 23:4; Rom. 8:28, 35–39; Phil. 3:7–11; 4:11, 12; 1 Pet.	Be there to comfort during illness and suffering.
Rejection by others	Ps. 22; 56; 94:14; 118:6; 1 Pet. 3:14, 15; 4:12–16	If there are things in the elderly that need changing, gently point them out and offer concrete suggestions as to how their attitudes could become different. Whether they are suffering for righteousness' sake or because of their own foolishness, clinging to God is an absolute necessity.
Failure, stupidity	Ps. 32:8, 9; 94:8–11; 1 Cor. 1:4–7, 18–31; 1 Cor. 2, 3	Foolish actions of the past must be laid aside and life lived in the present. Discern between true foolishness and the "foolishness" of the cross—which, in God's eyes, is true wisdom.

Antidotes to fear	Ps. 27; 33:18–22; Prov. 1:7; 3:5–8; 28:1, 14; Eccles. 12:13; Heb. 10:26–39; 1 John 1:5–10; 4:17–21	God is good, loving, wise, under-standing—and *perfect* in all these attributes. We should fear (i.e., respect) only him. There is nothing to fear when such a God cares for us.

SHARING MATERIALS

Scripture: Pss. 27, 33; Is. 41:10; 1 John 4:17–21
Hymns: Jesus, Lover of My Soul/Rock of Ages/How Sweet the Name of Jesus Sounds

See also charts on Death, Physical Decay, The Past, Comfort.

GRIEF

RELATED CONCERNS	BIBLE STUDY MATERIALS	´RESPONSE
Emotions	John 11 (esp. vss. 19, 31–38); Rom. 9:1ff.; 12:15; 2 Cor. 1, 2; 1 Thess. 4:13ff.	Be prepared for a whole range of emotions—hostility, fear, resentment, guilt, anger—as well as sadness. There *is* a proper way to express emotion.
Despair	Job 13:15; Ps. 42; 1 Thess. 4:13	Grief is sinful when it becomes despair. Learn from Job's comforters how to listen.
Sorrow	Job 2:10; Ps. 31:9ff.; 77; Prov. 14:13; 15:13; 17:22; 25:20; Is. 53:1–12; 35:10; Matt. 5:4	Jesus understands because he is well acquainted with grief. Let the sorrow of the elderly really sink into you—be sad with them. Explore the good things of the past, stressing God's goodness and faithfulness.
Looking ahead	Prov. 16:1, 3, 9; 2 Cor. 5:17; Phil. 3:13; 4:13; Rev. 21:1–5	A focus on Christ is essential if we are to look at the future without fear. Help the individual look for new possibilities of service to others. Set objectives and short-term goals. Reorganize life according to biblical principles.

SHARING MATERIALS

Scripture: Pss. 23, 42, 77; Is. 53:3, 4; 2 Cor. 1:3ff.; Phil. 4:13
Hymns: Be Still, My Soul/How Firm a Foundation/Man of Sorrows/Rock of Ages

See also charts on Comfort, Hope, Fear and other related areas.

HOPE

RELATED CONCERNS	BIBLE STUDY MATERIALS	RESPONSE
The need for hope: • despair, depression	Ps. 42	*Listen,* then respond.
• feeling forgotten or afflicted	Ps. 42; 39:7, 8	Be consistent in visitation. Show genuine deeds of love.
• grief	1 Cor. 15:19; 1 Thess. 4:13–18	See chart on Grief.
• weighed down by sin	Ps. 130	Help them confess, if appropriate; stress Christ's sufficiency. Actively exhort, instruct and confront problem areas—dealing with real problems in God's way brings real hope.
The basis of hope: • God's goodness	Jer. 17:7, 8 (cf. 17:5, 6); Eph. 1	Be realistic. Know God's promises and faithfulness.
• God's faithfulness	Ps. 146 (esp. vss. 5, 6; Lam. 3:22, 23	Share the gospel of hope. Pray with and for them.
• Christ	Eph. 2:12, 13; 1 Pet. 1:17–21	Read Scripture to them and encourage them to read on their
• Holy Spirit	Rom. 15:13	own.
• Scriptures	Rom. 15:4	
Building up hope: • Perseverance through trials	Ps. 40; Rom. 5:1–5; 15:4–6	Don't minimize present suffering. Acknowledge the struggle.
• Obedience	Ps. 31:23, 24; 119:113–120; Heb. 6:9–12; 1 Pet. 1:13ff.	Show how active obedience is possible—through right attitudes, continued prayer and giving of self for others—even in a nursing home!
• Waiting	Ps. 25; 27:14; 31:24; 62:5, 6	
Hope leads to faith	Heb. 11	Bring the familiar past to bear on the present. Reflect on God's goodness in the past.

SHARING MATERIALS

Scripture: Rom. 15:4, 5; 1 Cor. 15:19, 20; Titus 2:13; 1 John 3:1–3
Hymns: The Solid Rock

See also charts on Grief, Peace, The Past, Comfort.

THE PAST

RELATED CONCERNS	BIBLE STUDY MATERIALS	RESPONSE
Negative Concerns Sin	Ps. 25:7; Heb. 4:16; 2 Pet. 1:3–11; 1 John 1:9	A preoccupation with sin has only one cure—Christ! Stress the sufficiency of his death for every sin, no matter what it is.
Failure	Josh. 1:8; Ps. 107; Rom. 7; 8:28; Phil. 3:13, 14; 1 Pet. 1:13–21	In God's eyes we have all failed and deserve death—*but* Christ has borne that punishment. Past failures fade as God brings success in the present. How can you help an individual to be a success? Check Joshua 1:8.
Shame	Ps. 51; Rom. 6:21–23; 1 John 2:28	Much shame is connected with sin and failure; thus assurance of Christ's abiding love and presence is important.
Escape	Ex. 16:2, 3; Num. 11:4, 5; John 8:31–59	While some reminiscing is therapeutic, a refusal to live in the present and deal with its problems should be discouraged. Start by trying to relate to the person where he is; then try to draw him into the present.
Positive Concerns Meditation	Cf. Thought Life	Give positive material as input upon which they may meditate. Scripture portions, hymns, your personal experience—all these can be valuably shared.
Thanksgiving	Pss. 105, 106; Phil. 4:8, 9	Reflection on the *good* things of the past is an encouragement to the one reflecting and to anyone with whom these things are shared.
Encouragement	Ps. 77:11–20; Rom. 15:4	Scripture was given to us as an encouragement. Encouragement comes as we reflect upon God's goodness to his people.
Instruction to others	Ps. 71; 1 Cor. 10:11; Titus 2:3–5	The elderly should be encouraged to instruct young people by word and example.

Perspective on life	Phil. 3:1–16; 4:10–14	Reviewing the past (when one was healthy, strong, loved, etc.) is a necessary way of coping with the often dismal present.
Desire to be young again	Ps. 103:5; Is. 40:31	If possible, involve them in *activity*, especially with young people. "Borrow" a grade school class from a nearby school to show off costumes, give a program of skits and music—whatever. Youth is infectious, and many folks will feel younger just by being around the young.
Reality orientation	Heb. 12:1, 2	Involve them in your life and the life of the church. Use familiar songs and Scripture to help them relate past and present.

SHARING MATERIALS

Scripture: Phil. 3:13, 14; 4:4–13
Hymns: Faith of Our Fathers/How Firm a Foundation/Count Your Blessings

See also charts on Hope, Thought Life.

PEACE

RELATED CONCERNS	BIBLE STUDY MATERIALS	RESPONSE
Confusion/"senility"	Deut. 28:15–23, 28, 29, 50, 59, 61, 65, 66; Phil. 2:2, 5; 4:6, 7; Col. 3:15	Speak clearly, as if the person hears and understands you. Try to find a connecting thread in what he is saying and respond to that idea. See also "Senility."
Disobedience	Ps. 119:165; Is. 32:17; Rom. 8:6	If the person has a "grudge" against God, or is simply rebellious, he needs to be reminded of the necessity of coming to Christ to find peace.
Unrest	Ps. 23; 116:6, 7; 131; Matt. 11:28–30; John 10; Heb. 3, 4	No amount of positive thinking can substitute for resting in Jesus and trusting him to care for all our needs.
Trials and tribulation	Is. 43:1, 2; 54:11–17; John 16:33; Rom. 8:33–39; Rev. 3–5	If God is for us, who can be against us?
Disturbing personal relations	Eph. 4:1–3; Phil. 3:13, 14; Col. 3:12, 13; Heb. 12:1, 2, 14, 15	Encourage the elderly to do all they can on their side of any relationship to restore peace—and to pray for the other person(s) involved.
The road to peace	Is. 43; John 14:27; 16:33; Rom. 5:1; 14:17ff.; Gal. 5:22, 23; Eph. 2; Phil. 4:7, 8; Col. 3:15	Consult "Evangelism" for a description of how to share the gospel with the elderly. For those who are believers and need encouragement, see chart on Thought Life.

SHARING MATERIALS

Scripture: Ps. 8:4; 23; John 14:27; Phil. 4:7, 8
Hymns: Abide with Me/Peace, Perfect Peace/When Peace like a River/Leaning on the Everlasting Arms

See also charts on Companionship, Anxiety, The Past, Hope.

PHYSICAL DECAY

RELATED CONCERNS	BIBLE STUDY MATERIALS	RESPONSE
Weakness	Gen. 3; Ps. 84:5–7; 1 Cor. 15; 2 Cor. 4:5; 12:7–10; Rev. 21, 22	As much as you can, help the person to understand the process of physical aging—in relation to the curse of the fall, to the cross, *and* to the resurrection life. Be willing to assist physically, although it would be wise to consult the nursing staff first.
Failing sight	Is. 29:16–20	Approach directly and wear bright colors. Don't assume they are deaf as well! Remember, large-print literature is useful if they have some sight. Touch is very important.
Failing hearing	Is. 29:16–20; 42:18–20	Come close and use lower resonances rather then louder speaking. Speak directly into the ear, or perhaps write. Consider learning sign language if the person knows it. Again, *touch* is crucial.
Sickness	Is. 53; Jas. 5:10, 11, 16, 18	Don't stop visiting for fear that the sick may not want to see you. On the contrary, this is often a time of even greater isolation, and thus there is greater need for your comfort and strength and ability to discuss spiritual matters. Proceed as normally as possible, being careful not to overtax their strength. Be ready for sickness to bring on depression or thoughts of death.
Chronic invalidism	Rom. 5:3–5; 2 Cor. 4:6–18; 12:7–10; 1 Pet.	The chronic invalids, like the sick, perhaps need extra love and attention. Encourage them to do as much as they can do, and not despair. They are alive for a purpose—help them to discover it!

SHARING MATERIALS

Scripture: Ps. 84; 2 Cor. 4:5; 12:7–10
Hymns: A Mighty Fortress/Leaning on the Everlasting Arms

See also charts on Fear, Anxiety, Death, Self-Esteem, Hope.

SELF-ESTEEM

RELATED CONCERNS	BIBLE STUDY MATERIALS	RESPONSE
What God thinks of me	Gen. 1–3; Pss. 91, 139; Matt. 10:29–31; Rom. 3; 2 Cor. 5:17; Gal. 2:20; Eph. 1–3	Encourage a healthy view of man as created in God's image. Share passages that stress God's care for all his creatures and especially for Christians. BUT—be sure to show the fallen state of man, our unworthiness before God. And then—don't forget the hope that we have through salvation in Christ.
What I think of me	Job 10:1ff.; 14:1ff.; Ps. 22:6; 39; 102	Don't underestimate the deep feeling of insecurity and lack of self-worth. Listen—you may find you agree on some points—but remember that Christ offers hope in the situation.
What others think of me	Ps. 37; 40:14, 15; 102	See if the anxiety is justified (e.g., a chronic complainer may not be well liked). Work to a solution, always stressing the priority of acceptance by God over acceptance by others. Work to evaluate priorities—what is most important?

SHARING MATERIALS

Scripture: Ps. 139; 2 Cor. 5:17; Gal. 2:20
Hymns: Just As I Am/Have Thine Own Way, Lord

See also charts on Companionship, Peace, Time.

THOUGHT LIFE

RELATED CONCERNS	BIBLE STUDY MATERIALS	RESPONSE
Proper objects of thought	Ps. 27:4; 77; Rom. 8:5–8; 2 Cor. 4:18; Eph. 1:3–14; Phil. 4:8; Col. 3:1–4; Heb. 12:2; 1 Pet. 1:13	We can "set our minds" in various ways—through praise, worship of God, reading of Scripture, prayer, meditation on Scripture, prayer, fellowship with other Christians, sharing our faith with others. Help the elderly to engage in a variety of mind-setting activities. The best way to stop thinking about improper things is to fill the mind with good things. This should always involve meditation on Scripture. Help people make a list of eternal things—things to be thankful for. Involve them in sharing with others.
Combatting improper thought life	Rom. 7:19–25; 12:1, 2; Jas. 4; 1 Pet. 5:8, 9; 1 John	
Relating thought to action—"putting off and putting on"	Rom. 13:12–14; Eph. 4:22–32; Phil. 4:8, 9; Col. 3:8–17; Jas. 1:21, 22	Help structure their life with meaningful activity: visiting others, making things for others, or—if they are very sick—praying for various concerns of the home and the world. If they are doing good for others, they will be too busy to let their thoughts slip into dwelling on wrong things. Likewise, if their thoughts are proper, encourage them to show it—through cheerfulness, not complaining; through kind, not harsh, words; through sharing, not selfishness.

SHARING MATERIALS

Scripture: Ps. 103; Phil. 4:8; Col. 3:1–4
Hymns: May the Mind of Christ, My Savior/Jesus, the Very Thought of Thee/Jesus, Thou Joy of Loving Hearts

See also charts on Hope, Self-Esteem, Peace, Contentment, Anxiety, Time.

TIME

RELATED CONCERNS	BIBLE STUDY MATERIALS	RESPONSE
Proper use of time	Ps. 1; 31:15; 34:1–3; Eccles. 3:1–8; 1 Thess. 5:16–18	Encourage purposeful activity—helping others, reading, knitting, stuffing envelopes—all with a focus on glorifying God.
Motivation for using time properly	1 Cor. 3:11–15; 10:31; 15:58; Phil. 3:13, 14; Col. 3:23, 24; Heb. 6:10–12	God has a purpose for his children. *Whatever* a person can do is not wasted—even if he can "only" pray. Our time is not our own, it is God's. Our desire to please him should motivate us to use our time wisely.
Hindrances to using time properly (laziness, weariness, depression, disobedience)	Prov. 12:24, 27; 13:4; 15:19; 18:9; 26:13–16; Matt. 25:14–30; Gal. 6:2–10	At times, exhortation to leave behind laziness and disobedience may be necessary. Remember that you may be the *only* person encouraging the elderly to use their time wisely. Provide literature, suggest Christian radio as an alternative to television, encourage visitation within the home. For those not mobile, help them focus on passages of Scripture for meditation.

SHARING MATERIALS

Scripture: Prov. 26:13–16; 1 Cor. 10:31; 1 Thess. 5:16–18; Heb. 6:10–12
Hymns: Take My Life/O Jesus, I Have Promised

See also chart on Thought Life.

PART III

VISITATION

Visitation is at the heart of any nursing home ministry. In this part you will find numerous practical suggestions concerning a visitation ministry. Much of what you read is nothing more than common sense. But it is of great value to you to contemplate some of these commonsense guidelines and suggestions as you prepare for and evaluate your ministry of visitation. Use the margins and other white space to record your own observations and experiences. Take the opportunity this section provides you to become a self-conscious, teachable and—we hope—effective visitor of elderly people. The humble ministry of visitation is a ministry of great responsibility in the kingdom of God.

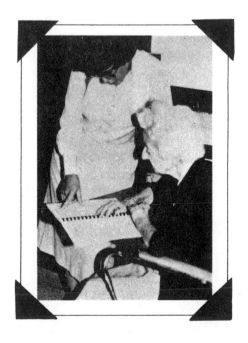

WHAT IS VISITATION?

When we consider visiting someone we tend to think of dropping in to say hello, or catching up on the latest news or just finding out how someone is. Our ideas of visiting often boil down to making a brief appearance or exchanging a few words.

The concept of visitation in the Bible is much more full and rich than our concept of "dropping by." To visit implies that one wishes to show concern and interest in another person. In Exodus 3, for example, we see God visiting Moses: "dropping by" in the form of a burning bush that promises to deliver the Israelites from bondage—through the one being visited, no less! The word for "visit" is also found in Psalm 8:4, where the wonder of a mighty God caring for insignificant man is discussed. In Matthew 25:36 visiting seems to imply caring for the needs of someone who is unable to care for himself. This idea is further elaborated in James 1:27, where doing what God commands is seen in terms of being like a father to the orphan, and a husband to a bereft wife. Visitation implies a deep commitment evidenced in a practical demonstration of Christ's love.

In the Scriptures God himself is often seen as a visitor. His visitation is his coming in blessing (Ruth 1:6; Jer. 29:10) and cursing (Lam. 4:22; Hos. 8:13). Likewise the coming of Christ is spoken of as a visitation that brings both blessing (Luke 1:68, 78; 7:16) and curse (Luke 19:44). The intention of his first visitation was gracious (John 3:17), although it resulted in judgment for the rebellious (John 9:39). His second coming or visitation (1 Pet. 2:12) will also be a time of blessing for the righteous and judgment for the wicked (2 Thess. 1:6–10).

During the time between Christ's two bodily visitations—we are told—our visitation should parallel his in significant ways (John 15:18–20; 1 John 4:17). The book of Acts, for example, is full of the deeds of the disciples as they visited various areas of their world, proclaiming the good news of Christ to many people. Although our purpose in visitation is always gracious, as Christ's was, it will inevitably result in judgment for the unbelieving (2 Cor. 2:14–16).

Love for Christ should be our supreme motivation for visitation of the elderly. Our concern and our desire to care for and protect depends on our love for the Christ who loves us (1 John 4:20). As we seek to learn more about visiting the elderly, let us remember that we are really learning more about loving God (Matt. 25:36, 40).

BASIC GUIDELINES FOR VISITATION

1. Be prepared:
   - Keep your personal relationship with God in good shape!
   - Seek support (prayer and fellowship) of other Christians.

2. Be sympathetic:
   - Cultivate a listening ear.
   - Hear what the person's needs are, not what you think they are.
   - Act in humility—don't think you are superior.

3. Be honest:
   - State why you have come.
   - Give the hope that you know—not false hope.

4. Be attentive:
   - Talk to individuals and learn their names.
   - Fix your attenton on what is being said *and* who is saying it.
   - Respond to questions and situations as well as you know how.
   - Involve yourself with people—not with impersonal, distant "problems."

5. Be open:
   - Share *yourself*—your hopes, fears, interests, even discouragements.
   - Be friendly, outgoing. Ask questions to start a conversation.

6. Be sensitive:
   - Accept the individual for who he is.
   - Encourage openness—don't monopolize the conversation.
   - Ask questions about what *this one person is* interested in—family, past employment, likes and dislikes (beware of entering into a "crab session"), friends, current events, God . . .

7. Be consistent:
   - Commit yourself to faithful visiting.
   - Continue in the face of boredom, discouragement or rejection—you are not visiting to meet your own needs, but to serve others in obedience to God.
   - Visit at appropriate times—not very late at night or early in the morning or around meal times (unless you are eating with some one person or helping to feed).

RELATING TO THE NURSING HOME STAFF

Most likely the first people you will meet at a nursing home are the staff. It is a privilege to be in the home and to show the love and concern of God to them as well as to the residents. A humble and courteous attitude to all staff will open many doors that might otherwise have remained closed. Such an attitude will help you to be seen as a blessing to the home, not a burden.

Administrator

When the occasion arises, introduce yourself. Spend time developing a good working relationship with the administrator and/or the assistant—as much as your schedules allow. Encourage them to share with you how they think you could best be of service in this home. Beware of giving the impression that you are there only to proselytize. Stress your desire to show love and friendship to the residents and to minister to their needs in the name of Christ.

Activity Director

Usually this person is the key contact in the home, especially for discovering the type of program needed—or desired—and the schedule of events to which you must adapt. (If there is no activity director, go to the administrator or the assistant.) Keep in touch with the activity director—how things are going, new ideas and problems from either side. Many homes require you to fill out a volunteer form and to sign in each time you visit. Use maturity and discernment as you share what you are doing. Don't unnecessarily bind your freedom by trying to do too much too quickly, by using religious clichés or by entering into arguments over religious matters. Sometimes a very "neutral" or nondenominational service or activity is wanted, and often it is possible to cooperate and give no cause for offense while still being true to the gospel as presented in Scripture. Compromise is not necessary, just wisdom.

Nurses

It is always good to check in with the nurse in charge when coming on to the floor, whether to visit or conduct a worship service or activity. Establish a relationship, exchange concerns and information, work together when possible, but be aware that nurses are often genuinely busy, particularly during changes of shift. Be especially courteous and respectful of them and their time. Do take to them questions of care and concern, including residents' complaints. But remember, you may not have all the facts. Sometimes theirs is the responsibility of supervising and directing an uncooperative staff. You can help by being a peacemaker. Serious conflicts need to be taken to the supervisor or director of nursing.

Nursing Assistants

The most in number on the staff, nursing assistants have much contact with residents and much possibility for genuine care. Often they are very helpful to visitors. Many may come to worship services in the home. If they do, notice them and include them in the audience. Talk with them; provide spiritual care, comfort, support and counsel for them too. Remember their families and their personal concerns in prayer. If they are unruly, uncooperative or disruptive during a worship service or an activity, speak to them about it with humility. If they persist, speak to the activities director.

Housecleaning Staff

These people are not involved officially with the residents, though they do have considerable contact with them and can be very helpful in encouraging them. Pray for this part of the staff and support them in their work.

Kitchen Staff

Do not interfere with meal times. Try to be helpful but be sure to ask a nurse or assistant about it first. Sometimes our "helping" gets in the way, but often the staff are most appreciative of some assistance, e.g., feeding a patient. In some places, helping with food or feeding residents is illegal. Be sure to find out from the nurse if the resident is on any special dietary restrictions before bringing in food.

THE ART OF CONVERSATION

For many people one of the biggest fears about visiting in nursing homes revolves around the question: "What will I talk about?" With some people you visit this won't be a problem. They will do much of the talking, and you will find yourself listening to a steady stream of questions, reminiscences and the like! But your visit with other nursing home residents may be something quite unusual. Many elderly people sit for hours—even for days on end—scarcely speaking a word or being spoken to. For them, there is little to stimulate either their minds or their bodies. Thus it may be up to you to carry the conversation.

We have found that those people who find it difficult to lead a conversation need not fear the challenge of conversing with nursing home residents. It is very common that the people we visit are so happy to have someone talk to them that they don't care what the topic is or how often the topic changes. This gives the visitor great freedom in choosing topics and talking about things that he is familiar with. Through many years of using this freedom we have come to make the following suggestions.

Listening shows that you really care and accept who the person is. A good listener learns about the other person's interests, hopes, needs and desires and gains insights for being helpful in these areas. Plan to develop your skills as a listener.

Don't respond to feelings with facts alone. Let yourself feel what the person is going through. Genuine sympathy (feeling with someone) makes good communication possible. You will find that a mutual friendship will grow naturally out of a sympathetic relationship.

Avoid questions that can be easily answered with a simple yes or no. One-word answers stifle conversation in a hurry. Questions that seek explanations allow the other person to teach you something about himself. As he does this, be careful not to probe too deeply on the first visit. There may be sensitive areas that you should avoid until you know the person much better.

These are some topics about which you may want to converse:

The Surroundings

1. The room—cards on display, plants, pictures, furniture, view out the window, roommate, arts and crafts, television program, music, color of decor.
2. The home—food, nurses, visitors, friends, sitting room, noise level. Although such topics may provide an excuse for some to vent their complaints, we think that such opportunity can be important and valuable in getting to know the person and showing your concern for him. Do not, how-

ever, encourage sinful attitudes; instead, encourage constructive evaluation and positive, responsible involvement.

Family History

1. The past—where they grew up, number in family, favorite family pastimes, favorite sports, travel, school, where they have lived, what it was like back then, job of parents, jobs they have held.
2. The present relationships—married? how long? spouse's name, children's names, where they live, whether they visit, any grandchildren?

General

Weather, recent events in the news, how their week was; activities in the past week in the home, in the week to come?

Spiritual Concerns

What church they attended, what it meant to them. Did they like singing? Favorite hymns, faith of their parents, how they think of God, what they pray about, how they think of Jesus Christ.

THE VISITOR AND HIS RESOURCES

We have previously mentioned several necessary personal qualifications of the visitor. Here, in more detail, are three key resources which the visitor has at his fingertips—himself, the Scripture and prayer.

The Use of Self

You are one of your big resources as a visitor! Look to God for help as you strive to become a person who is more and more fitted to serve. The following characteristics—humility, vulnerability, commitment, empathy and the capability of listening—these are of special importance in a nursing home ministry.

Humility
If we have a proper sense of self, then we will not suffer from either pride or false humility. This will enable us to be ourselves and allow the elderly to be themselves. How can we actually be humble? By recognizing that we don't have all the answers, expecting to learn from others. By treating them as if they are worthwhile—because they are!

Vulnerability
To the extent that we know ourselves and have a proper sense of worth, we can open up to others—and to the possibility of rejection, criticism, pain and sacrifice as well as to the possibility of pleasure and praise. As we share thoughts, feelings and hopes with others, they see us as "human too" and will more readily open up to us.

Commitment
If we are not willing to sustain a deep level of relationship with a person as long as *he* needs it, then we are not letting ourselves be used as fully as we could. It is through our *continued* humility and vulnerability and our *continued* empathy and listening that we really care for the individual.

Empathy
This process involves both our mind and our heart. To empathize we must be able to understand what is happening to the individual, feel sympathy for what he's going through and then put the two together in helping him deal with the situation.

Listening
Much of the above takes for granted that we know how to listen. Listening is an art that is not always as easy as it seems. Listening . . .
- *expresses love.* It recognizes the importance of the individual. It shows a willingness to spend time and energy on another's behalf.
- *brings understanding.* This takes time—there usually are no instant

solutions to problems and no shortcuts around the need for personal sharing. Whether it's a person or a situation that we're endeavoring to understand, listening requires giving up our own interests and concentrating fully and actively on his (Phil. 2:3, 4).

- *participates actively.* Listening is not merely not talking. It encourages the other person to say more, without prying; it seeks to formulate a response, without thinking of self; and it strives to hear what is *not* said as well as to understand what is said.

"Listen to me, do but listen, and let that be the comfort you offer me" (Job 21:2 NEB).

The Use of Scripture

While the resource of self is often unreliable and imperfect, the Scriptures offer a stability and hope to which both we and the elderly can turn. In a changing, fragmented world, the word of God directs our attention to a perfect God who never changes and who can put order and meaning into our lives.

When to use the Scriptures
1. Find an appropriate time.

Referring to Scripture too soon can give the impression the Bible has only pat (and therefore irrelevant) answers. Referring to it too late makes it seem like an afterthought. Be sure you really understand—then share Scripture. Remember Job's comforters!

2. Comfort the suffering.

A word of comfort in the context of personal relationship, and at the right time, can be a deep blessing. Often the purpose and meaning of suffering need to be seen.

3. Meet their needs.

Don't read Scripture merely to meet your own needs; nor should you read your problems into their situation. But be ready to share Scripture through which God has spoken to you, if it is fitting.

4. Respond to the Holy Spirit.

Don't share from the Bible out of a sense of duty or compulsion. Let the Holy Spirit be your guide.

How to use the Scriptures
1. Select the appropriate content.

Your choice should be guided by the residents' needs—give yourself time to find out their needs. Some of these needs are discussed in the charts found in Part II.

2. Help the person to identify with Scripture.

Share passages with which the individual can identify. This helps self-acceptance before God and enables him to express himself.

3. Choose the appropriate translation.

For residents who are versed in the Bible, you might stay with the familiar or expected (usually KJV). For those who are unfamiliar with the Bible, consider using a modern version—one they can read with ease.

4. Share with one another.

Let *them* share with you what they are learning from Scripture and their experience. But feel free, also, to share what God has been teaching you.

Suggested Scripture passages
1. Forgiveness—Pss. 32, 51, 103; Is. 1:18; 53:4-6; Mic. 7:18-20; Rom. 8:1-4; Heb. 4:15, 16; 1 John 1:6-10
2. Comfort—Pss. 4, 23, 116; Is. 40:28-31; 41:10; 43:1-5; Matt. 11:28; Rom. 8:35-39
3. Hope—Pss. 42, 139, 145; Rom. 5:1-5; 1 Cor. 15; 1 John 3:1-3; Rev. 21:1-8
4. Love—Deut. 7:6-10; Is. 43:1-4; John 3:16-18; 14; 15:9-17; 17:9-26
5. Trust—Ps. 23; 37:3-7; John 14:26, 27; 2 Cor. 4:16-18; Phil. 4:4-7; Heb. 12:12-15; 1 Pet. 1:13-21

The Use of Prayer

Prayer is another great resource since it taps into our greatest resource of all—God. Our prayers are important, not just as a comfort to the person we are praying with, but as a communication with the living God who hears and *answers*. In prayer we not only draw close to God but to one another.

When to pray
1. Find an appropriate time.

For each resident the appropriate time may be different. It is important not to pray with someone before adequate communication has taken place. Then the prayer can reflect to God the concerns that have come out of a conversation. One must be careful not to use prayer to end conversation. It may well be that after a time of prayer you will want to continue a conversation. Often deep feelings are triggered in response to talking with God. Be willing to stay and respond to these thoughts and feelings.

2. Be alert to "anxious times."

Pray before potentially stressful situations such as surgery, tests, unfamiliar changes.

3. Strengthen believers' faith.

Pray with those who show some evidence (verbal, written material, etc.) of faith.

4. Examine your motives.

Ask: Am I praying to meet *my* needs or theirs? Have their needs in the forefront of your mind—often God will give an added blessing by ministering to you too!

How to pray
1. Focus on God.

Praise God for who he is and what he has done—prayer and supplication *with thanksgiving.*

2. Focus on needs.

Focus on what you think the individual would want prayed for—health, friendship, finances. Discern his hopes, fears and desires.

3. Adjust to the person's background.

Be aware of the denominational and ethnic background and adjust your style of prayer accordingly (e.g., formal vs. informal).

4. Expect God to respond.

Only by expecting God to respond can you teach others that prayer is real and is heard by God.

5. Give resurrection hope.

The power of the resurrected Christ is active both in this life and the life to come. Help the person to see that power as active in his life.

6. Be concise.

Remember that the elderly often have a shortened attention span, so keep your prayers short.

The material in this section ("The Visitor and His Resources") is adapted from *Spiritual Care: The Nurse's Role* by Sharon Fish and Judith Allen Shelly. © 1978 by Inter-Varsity Christian Fellowship of the USA and used by permission of InterVarsity Press, Downers Grove, Ill. 60515, USA.

GUIDELINES FOR THE FIRST FEW VISITS

The following pages are meant to be guidelines. Since the first visits are often the most difficult, it is good to be as spiritually and psychologically prepared as possible. However, don't be bound to the suggestions outlined below. Read through the next few pages, meditate, pray and open your heart to various possibilities.

There is no need to try to remember numerous details. After reading and meditating on this section, be free to branch out on your own—trusting God to prepare you, to guide you and to give you the flexibility you will need for the particular situation you encounter.

Pre-Visit Preparation

Before you go to the nursing home for the first time, and in successive visits as well, ask yourself the following questions:
1. Have I taken time to pray?
   - for myself, what I will do and say
   - for those I am about to meet
   - for the staff of the home
   - for others going with me
2. Do I have a goal?
   - help write a letter
   - talk about God
   - chat with three people
   - lead a worship service
3. Do I have the material I need?
   - Bible, tracts
   - games, puzzles
   - small gift(s)
   - writing materials
   - musical instrument
4. How do I look? How do I feel?
   - dress—usually not-too-casual is appropriate
   - cheerfulness—would someone want to talk to me?
   - motives—am I trying to serve God? to serve the elderly?
   - breath—in all likelihood many will be hard of hearing and I'll have to talk "close up"

The First Visit

Contact the nurse in charge of the unit you are visiting. It is wise to have your presence officially recognized, although that may not always be necessary. There may also be a check-in point at the front desk or in the activities office. Find out the rules and abide by them. Although checking in may seem unnecessary after a while, contact with those in charge not only is a courtesy to them, but also provides an opportunity for you to find out who is sick, depressed, lonely and in special need of a visitor.

When arriving at the door of an individual's room be sure to knock and await permission to enter; or enter slowly and tentatively, especially if the person is hard of hearing. This is probably the only private space this person has—don't violate his control over it.

You may wish to begin visitation by meeting the person in an open lounge. This setting is also good for general conversation, but often presents too many distractions for deeper, more personal talk.

Introduce yourself and start a light, friendly conversation. Tell the person a little about yourself—your name, relationship to the home, and some possible background in common, such as job, church or family. If you have no such common background with the individual, just state your purpose in visiting. Be honest, concerned and direct.

The environment in which the resident lives is very important, not only for its effect on him but for what it tells you about him. The external situation (the room, other people, noise, flowers, the person's physical condition) can open up areas for conversation, as well as give clues to the internal condition (mental, spiritual state) of the person you are visiting. Be prepared to adapt your goals to the needs—but don't necessarily abandon your purposes altogether!

Though you do have a decidedly spiritual interest in these elderly people, beware of focusing too much—even exclusively, perhaps—on "religious" things. Be ready to be involved in the whole of life.

Leave any literature that may be helpful in a particular situation. This may not always be appropriate, for example, with some Jewish people, with those who cannot understand or with those who cannot read English. In such cases it would be better to let your words and actions leave the lasting impression.

If possible, tell the people you visit when they may expect you next. Don't get carried away and promise more than you can realistically do. Faithfulness to your word is especially important to those who have so little on this earth to look forward to. If you do say you will return at a certain time on a certain day and are unable to make it at the specified time, be sure to call the home and leave a message or ask to speak to the person directly on the phone.

After you leave, write reminder notes, reflect on your visit and pray. As you await your next visit, make a note of any Scripture that may apply to the person's situation, and meditate on it, praying for wisdom as to how and when to help meet his needs. Ask others to pray for you and your "new friend"—this is a great way to involve others in the ministry to the elderly! Make some tentative plans for your next and following visits, including the possibility of relating to the individual's family or involvement in other activities.

The Second Visit

Be sure you have reviewed your notes from the first visit. Pray and meditate on the response you think would be appropriate for the visit. Follow the same basic procedure as you did in the first visit, noting especially the following:

1. Be ready for any changes that may have occurred—new roommate, death of a friend, good or bad news, change of mood, and so on. Adapt the response you *thought* would be right to fit the new situation. Don't hold to a rigid agenda, but be flexible.
2. Enter again with an introduction that assumes neither too little nor too much recognition. Give gracious clues to your identity as needed. Stimulating people to remember provides good mental exercise and helps establish a proper sequence and time-consciousness. There may be some resistance to this due to laziness, neglect and/or physiological disability. As best you can, try to decide which of these reasons applies. Don't push too hard for fast recall, whatever the cause.
3. Try to undo any misunderstanding that may have arisen from the first visit. And plan not to repeat your early mistakes. Did you monopolize the conversation? Be prepared to listen more. Did you come across too forcefully in sharing the gospel? Be more sensitive this time. Were you too informal with someone from a more formal background? Be more adaptable—and apologize if it's appropriate.

The Third and Following Visits

As you spend more time with an individual you may not feel the need to take notes. If you're spending a fair amount of time (twenty to thirty minutes at least) with your friend, note taking is probably not necessary. If, however, you are visiting a large number of people for short periods of time, it's probably best to stick with a few notes in order to keep everyone straight in your mind. Be guided by your own needs.

The following hints are offered as suggestions. They are by no means exhaustive nor meant to be followed with strict rigidity.

1. Since elderly people are close (relatively speaking) to death, and some may be sick and actually very near dying, make every visit count. Be there for the person—give each one your full, loving attention.

2. As before, don't leave false expectations about what you can or might do, or when you might visit again.
3. Move toward dealing with particular problems or concerns. If confrontation or exhortation is needed, be sure you have established a sufficient basis of trust and friendship first.
4. Encourage spiritual examination and life review (i.e., meditation on past life, its successes and failures, with a view to dealing with unresolved feelings or conflicts). Move toward a continuing program of personal, meaningful examination of self—issuing in service to God and others. Avoid dwelling on the past that can't be changed; concentrate on learning from mistakes and improving present attitudes and behavior.
5. Seek ways other than visits to be involved in their lives and to involve them in your life. Consider their needs and plan constructively and creatively to meet these needs. This may mean writing letters for them, taking them to a potluck, arranging transportation to a church service—the possibilities are endless. What would they like to do? What are they able to do with help?

SPECIAL SITUATIONS

Those Who Have Visitors Already

Occasionally when you go to visit an individual, someone else will already be there visiting. Normally you should give way to such prior visitors, although you may wish to get acquainted and talk with them if they seem open to conversation. You should be especially eager to meet your friend's family members, who have so much influence on the nursing home resident. As the occasion arises, introduce yourself, keeping in mind that there may be needs in the family (economic, social, spiritual) to which you may wish to respond.

Those Who Are Blind or Have Limited Vision

Approach the blind person directly and speak to him face to face. Don't assume that because he has difficulty seeing, he also cannot hear. Don't shout; use a normal speaking voice but speak clearly, slowly and distinctly. Touch can be important to a blind person, but speak before you touch him or you may startle him.

Remember the importance of other senses to a blind person—such as smell and touch. For example, if you are bringing a bouquet of flowers let him smell and touch them. Describe things from the environment and your own experience for the person.

If a person is not totally blind, wear bright colors. Bright lipstick may help to facilitate lip reading. Large-print literature is also helpful. (See "Physical Decay" in Part II and "Large-Print Literature," Appendix B.)

Those Who Are Deaf or Hard of Hearing

If the person you visit is totally deaf, consider writing or signing as alternatives to verbal communication. It is usually best with the totally deaf to stand facing them so they can see your facial expressions and read your lips. Touching the person gently is a good way of attracting his attention to you before you begin speaking. Touch is also important for the hard of hearing.

If a person is hard of hearing find out which ear is the "good" ear. Sometimes you may have to speak directly into his ear, but normally standing or sitting on the good side is sufficient. Does he have a hearing aid? Is it turned on? Are the batteries working?

When you speak, speak slowly, distinctly, simply and at a slow-to-moderate rate of speed. Lower resonances communicate better than greater volume. If you must speak more loudly than normal, be aware that your voice carries and take into account others within earshot.

Those Who Are Very Sick

People who are seriously ill are most likely to be bedfast. They too appreciate and need visits. However, do not overtax them; check with the nurses on their condition. Do not stay too long, or demand participation on their part. They may be too weak or in too much pain to communicate verbally. Be alert to eye communication. A gentle touch and few words may be the best expression of love. Words of comfort and assurance and a brief prayer are often quite appropriate.

Those Who Shout

Try to decide what the reason for the shouting is. The person may be deaf or hard of hearing, or in need of attention of either a medical or personal sort. There may be a legitimate need that is being ignored. He may have genuine spiritual problems related to unresolved grief or loneliness, for example. In that case, he may be "crying for help." On the other hand, this person may be sinfully selfish, totally self-centered. It would be best to speak directly to him about this. Respond appropriately to your own understanding of the situation. A gentle touch and the assurance of your presence and care are again very important.

Those Who Want to Cling to You Physically

Physical touch is very important in communicating the concern and love you feel for the elderly people in the nursing home. You will observe that it is virtually a universal need among them, but in some instances you may need to deal with the *excessive* "needs" of some individuals. Be alert to potential difficulties and handle them in such a way as to keep a proper balance—expressing of genuine caring, but not acceding to improper overtures.

Those Who Have Religious Beliefs or Come from Denominations Other Than Your Own

Inevitably, you will differ with some residents in religious matters. First of all try to determine whether there is genuine Christian faith. Genuine Christian faith can come to expression in a variety of ways; do not be judgmental of those who simply have chosen a different form of expression. However, there are essentials on which all Christians must be in agreement, for example, Jesus is Lord, Jesus is the Son of God, Jesus died for the sins of his people and has been raised from the dead (1 Cor. 15:3, 4). It is best not to enter into discussion of controversial matters (such as mode of baptism) unless there is substantial agreement on such basics. Often controversy is most wisely avoided in favor of rejoicing together in our common salvation and the goodness of God.

Those Who Do Not Speak English

Not all elderly residents of a nursing home will have English as their primary language, of course, so if it is possible you should arrange for someone who does speak their language to visit them. If you do visit, speak in very simple English. Familiar passages of Scripture (e.g., the Lord's Prayer, Psalm 23, John 3:16, the name "Jesus") may be helpful in establishing communication.

Touch is as always important. Printed literature can also be useful since some people who can not speak or understand spoken English can read some English words. (See Appendix B, "Large-Print Literature.") Bibles and other religious literature are also available in other languages.

Those Who Always Complain

When a resident complains, first be sure you have really listened to him. Try to see things from his perspective. If the complaint is valid, perhaps there is something you can do to help. Avoid becoming involved beyond what you are equipped to handle as this will mean disappointment and discouragement for both of you. Respond realistically! Often a sympathetic ear or a word from Scripture is a great comfort. At all cost, avoid pat answers. If an individual persists in complaining during every visit, feel free to speak up about his attitudes, but don't be condemnatory. As you encourage the person to change, be sure your love for him shines through.

SENILITY

When we hear the word *senility* we often think of confusion and disorientation as to time and place, hopelessness, lack of self-care, forgetfulness, inability to carry out everyday tasks, second childhood and impairment of intellectual functions. And usually we consider all these things to be the inevitable price of old age.

While such symptoms are often present among residents of nursing homes, it is unfair and unwise to brand those who display these characteristics with the term "senility." Dr. Arthur Frese, in his book *The End of Senility* (New York: Arbor House, 1978) states that the term senility has no real medical legitimacy; that it is not used in any diagnostic nomenclature; in fact, that there is no such disease as senility. He is convinced that this word and its use is the result of prejudice against the elderly which he terms "ageism." What is often termed senility reflects a failure and refusal of diagnosticians to carry out a thorough diagnosis.

There are two classes of mental impairment: functional and organic. Functional impairment is often the result of depression. Organic impairment, which means actual impairment of the brain tissue itself, is termed organic brain syndrome (OBS). Organic brain syndrome may be acute, resulting from causes such as malnutrition, misuse of drugs, pneumonia and thyroid conditions—to name just a few. As such it may be responsive to medical care; it may be temporary and reversible. Without care this acute condition may become one of four chronic OBS diseases from which approximately one-half of all American nursing home patients suffer.

Though the symptoms of senility may have organic causes, it is often difficult to determine whether they are the result of OBS or simply the depression, loneliness, grief, guilt, loss of self-esteem, indifference from others, and feelings of uselessness to which the elderly are often subject. When visiting nursing homes, therefore, we must be prepared not to attempt to judge the medical condition of the apparently senile, but to respond to the emotional and spiritual needs as best we can discern them.

Responding to the spiritual state of the senile person may mean recognizing that his condition could be a result of a life devoted to disobedience to God's commands (see Deut. 28:21–24, 47–50, 58–61, 65 and 30:7). To this distressing situation we can bring the grace and mercy of Christ who became a curse for us (Gal. 3:13, 14).

RELATING TO THOSE WHO ARE SENILE

The goal in relating to a person who appears to be senile is the same as with any person: to establish a meaningful relationship. Special care needs to be taken with those who seem senile since they do not always understand or respond to our idea of a normal conversation. Here are some suggestions for making conversation with those who are confused or disoriented.

1. Try to engage the individual in conversation about present realities. Talk about matters of concern *now*, for example, your presence and the purpose of your visit, or about activities around the home. Perhaps you might even venture to topics about the community or nation or world. Gain his attention and interest, then build on a present theme. This approach is quite often unsuccessful, but surely worth a try. Usually the initial exchange will be sufficient to determine whether such an approach will work.

2. Join the person where he is. Usually the confused person will talk about seemingly unrelated realities, often about events in the distant past. These events can be even more real to him than your presence. As best you can, step into the scene as he presents it to you. Ask questions about the situation being described. Keep your stance in "present reality" and give counsel into the situation as if it were indeed a present happening. Often bitterness, resentment, hostility or hurt is keeping the individual tied to the past. If so, speak directly to him regarding this, counseling about forgiveness and mercy.

3. Recall with the person something that has been meaningful to him in the past. If you know a little about his past, reminisce about a favorite job, hobby or friend. Often a reference to spiritual realms will touch something deep inside and give a focus for thoughts and feelings. The Twenty-third Psalm, the Lord's Prayer, other Scripture or familiar hymns can be most successfully used. Often the person will join in reciting or singing along with you and regain orientation to a remarkable degree.

4. Don't be surprised if a person bursts into tears at the reading of Scripture or even the mention of God or prayer. For many you are probably the first person in a *very* long time who has shown such concern about them.

5. In general, genuine love and concern communicate more loudly than words. Physical touch is very important, since it shows that you consider the individual to be a person.

6. Prayer can be very effective, especially if it is short, concise and relevant to the person's needs and desires.

7. Continue your efforts at establishing relationship, regardless of any lack of response or of progress. When possible, do share the gospel, even if there seems to be no communication established. John 3:16 is especially appropriate, and can be spoken even when the person seems to be in another world, as it were. Leave the rest to God.

INTRODUCING SOMEONE NEW TO VISITATION

As you become involved in some aspect of ministering to the institutionalized elderly, you will no doubt desire to have other people involved with you as co-workers. Visiting older people is one activity that many feel drawn to and equipped for and is something in which you can always use assistance. Even the most outgoing person, however, may have some hesitations and reservations about visiting in a nursing home. The following, then, are some suggestions for introducing someone new to a rich, rewarding experience in visitation.

1. Obtain as much relevant information as possible from the prospective visitor, beforehand. Try to discover what kinds of people he might naturally fit in with at the home—common interests, language, needs, experience, etc. Look for impediments to visiting—fears (find the source), doubts, bad past experiences.
2. Communicate something about what will likely happen (the bad as well as the good), but not too much. Leave room for discovery and dependence on God.
3. Discuss the details of visitation—matters of dress, manners, basic rules and policies of the home—as well as your goals and procedure.
4. Pray with the person if possible—at least for him and for the necessary arrangements.
5. Be in charge. Take the person with you. Let him observe you and lean on you during the first visit.
6. Go to the familiar "comfortable" spots first. Don't initiate a situation threatening to either the new visitor or the residents.
7. Be sensitive to the visitor's reactions—i.e., discomfort, repulsion, enjoyment, eagerness. Keep encouraging him to share his feelings with you.
8. Help him to recognize the part he can play in the visitation program. Give him opportunity and the freedom to respond in his own way.
9. Discuss freely with him the degree to which he prefers to lean on you for support and guidance or to take initiative and find his own place.

PART IV

WORSHIP AND EVANGELISM

In addition to visitation, Christians have an opportunity to serve older persons in nursing homes as they help them to worship God and study the Bible, and as they share the good news of Jesus Christ with them. In this part you will be given a number of practical suggestions as to how you might organize and implement a program of worship and evangelism.

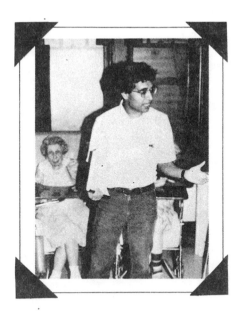

WORSHIP

Worship of God is an often neglected aspect in the lives of the institutionalized elderly. Yet worship can and should play an important part in their lives. Not only can they offer God the praise and honor he deserves, but they can also derive deep satisfaction, joy and peace through worship of him.

Because of the varied backgrounds of people in nursing homes, there are many types of worship services that can be appropriate. On the one hand there is the very formal liturgical service; on the other, the informal, flexible and sometimes improvised service. This second type is more usual in homes where the residents have limited alertness and difficulty participating in or following a fixed service.

In either situation there is likely to be a variety of religious backgrounds (Roman Catholic, Baptist, Presbyterian, etc.) as well as ethnic backgrounds (Ukrainian, black, white . . .). Some blend of traditions, therefore, is recommended—a variety in type of hymn and style of prayer, for example—in order to give the most people something to which they can relate from their own past experience. Touch on the familiar whenever possible—Bible stories, old hymns, the Lord's Prayer, the doxology. Focus on the basics of Christianity—Christ, his death for sin and resurrection to give new life. Avoid unnecessary controversy. Work toward simplicity yet don't be afraid to exercise their minds.

INITIATING A WORSHIP SERVICE

Pick a time of day for the service, in consultation with the activities director and nursing staff, that will avoid interrupting meal times, medicine distribution, other planned activities or times when residents may be especially tired. Staff are often helpful in suggesting who might like to come to the services and may assist in gathering people from their rooms. If not, allow enough time before the service to remind people to come and to bring those in wheelchairs. Consider visiting rooms regularly before the service to extend personal invitations, introduce yourself and generally acquaint yourself with the home.

Finding a good location within the home for the service can be a problem. Often the home will have no special chapel area, nor even a separate room that could be used for services. If this is the case, you will probably find that a general lounge area is available—sometimes with a built-in audience! If you do use a general open area, be tactful and courteous as you turn off the television, rearrange furniture as necessary and otherwise transform a lounge into a chapel. Remember that many of these people cannot move independently—and they may wish they could. Be gentle and humble in your approach, but don't let negative reactions deter you from your purpose. If necessary, help move those who don't wish to be involved in the service to a new location.

Often the location for the service is one where it is impossible for everyone to see and hear, if the leader simply stands in one place. Sometimes furniture and/or people can be rearranged. If the changes are quite extensive, assume that you will be doing the moving yourself, but check with the staff first. Be sure to express your gratitude to staff members who help you set up. This encourages them and makes you an asset rather than a burden.

If you are unable to rearrange the furniture satisfactorily, you must plan to have your leader move about so that he can be seen by all the participants. Move slowly and as naturally as possible. Don't be surprised or "thrown off" by someone wanting to touch you as you pass. Try to minister to this need in a way that doesn't detract from the service. A squeeze on the hand is often enough, or a brief word of acknowledgment. Or perhaps you can hold the person's hand for several minutes as you continue the service.

The worship leader and all those who have a part in the service must be sensitive to those who are hard of hearing. It is not inappropriate to ask whether anyone is having difficulty hearing. Once you have determined what your volume level ought to be, try to maintain it.

SUGGESTED FORM OF WORSHIP
(Total time: 30–45 minutes)

Introduction

Introduce yourself and the worship time, making a transition from other activities.

Call to Worship

A psalm (such as Ps. 95 or 100) is useful here.

Invocation

Your opening prayer should be clear, authoritative and short.

Songs

Singing brings involvement and awakens past experiences of worship. Instruments (piano, guitar, flute, etc.) can be profitably used, especially if the leader has trouble directing in singing. Requests for favorites may be included here.

Scripture

Scripture may be read at this point or during your message. Many worship leaders prefer to use the King James Version since it is what many elderly people are accustomed to.

Message

This should not be a full-scale sermon. Ten to fifteen minutes in length should be sufficient.

Prayer

This prayer is the counterpart of what is often termed the "pastoral prayer." Pray for residents in the home, and with them for others. Requests may be taken, but note what is said in "Participation in a Worship Service" (see next section). Remember too that much training in intercession can be done by example.

The Lord's Prayer

Because this prayer is familiar, it can well be used as a prayer in unison at the close of the previous prayer.

Songs

Depending on the time available (e.g., if your talk was quite brief), circumstances (e.g., no scheduled activities follow the service) and alertness or eagerness of the residents, more singing may be appropriate.

Closing

Close with a brief prayer and scriptural blessing (e.g., Jude 24, 25; Heb. 13:20, 21; 2 Cor. 13:14 and/or the doxology).

We have found it worthwhile to announce at the beginning of the service that we are willing to talk or pray with individuals after the service. Those who have a desire to share their extensive needs and deep-felt emotions during the service will then be satisfied to wait. After the service we ask those who wish prayer—or who just need to talk—to raise their hands.

We have also noticed in the homes we have visited, the desire of many individuals to receive Holy Communion. The elderly are often overlooked in this area of the church's spiritual life. Perhaps a way to overcome this is to arrange for a minister to come, asking individuals to indicate, during the week before, their desire to receive communion. Take down names and go to individual rooms with the minister to provide a link with the worship services you have been conducting. If individuals express privately their desire for Holy Communion, ask appropriate ministers of their denomination to come to them whenever possible. Churches should also be encouraged to transport the elderly to their communion services.

PARTICIPATION IN A WORSHIP SERVICE

Participation by persons other than the leader is very helpful. Since the elderly often are like small children with respect to attention span and interest, activity during the service promotes alertness and attention. This is true whether the activity comes from people you bring with you, or from those within the home. Beware, however, of precipitating confusion and disorder through too much activity or by means of changes that occur too quickly.

Participation by People from Outside the Home

Use the many gifts that others have been given by having them lead in song or prayer, give their testimony, read Scripture or do whatever they feel confident enough to do. Assistants are invaluable for providing help with hymnbooks (both distribution and finding the hymns during the service) as well as functioning as troubleshooters for the possible interruptions that may occur. Children can be of considerable help in certain tasks and usually are appreciated by the residents.

Participation by Residents in the Nursing Home

Feel free to ask the staff, residents and even visitors to participate if they wish. Often there are staff members who are free to listen and even join in. They may respond to your suggestions by singing, praying, sharing a testimony or otherwise encouraging the residents.

If you want to give some of the residents an opportunity to contribute something to the service, think over the following questions: Will the contribution be heard? (Repeating what is said, will help.) Will the contribution be an aid to worship? (Am I ready to handle in public what may be deep personal concerns such as "I want to die," "Someone stole my money" and "I hate it here"?) Will the contribution be significant and edifying? (Would controversial and relatively insignificant points of view be disclosed which would be difficult to include in worship?)

Participation from the residents is quite valuable. Their worshipful, controlled participation is a great blessing. It is important to bring them into the service as much as is possible. But as you do so, be ready to handle problems should they arise.

DEALING WITH INTERRUPTIONS IN A SERVICE

In any nursing home, no matter where or when you are holding a service there may be interruptions. These could come in the form of wandering visitors, residents or staff, or as talking, shouting or even arguing among those attending the worship service. Obviously you must either recognize the interruption within the context of worship or ignore it. The following suggestions may also be helpful.

Interruptions by Residents

In the case of loud outbursts or irrelevant interference, it is best if someone not leading the service quietly attends to the problem. Often a few soft, direct words along with a light touch (a hand on the shoulder, for example) will restore calm. If you are alone, or if the outburst persists, you yourself may need to say or do something. Feel free to ask the staff to remove the person if the service is continually disrupted.

Interruptions by Staff

When it is a staff member who is noisy, inconsiderate and disruptive—be forbearing! Indicate before the service in a gentle, humble manner that you are about to conduct a worship service and would appreciate their cooperation. In some cases, someone may need to remind them during the service. We have found that most staff members are willing to cooperate *if* they are approached in a humble manner. If problems persist, however, feel free to speak to the activities director or the nurse in charge. Remember, by now you have cleared your presence with the authorities and have their backing. Use this clout if you need to, so that God may be worshiped and glorified and the needs of the residents may be met.

Interruptions by Visitors

We have found most visitors to be very sensitive and cooperative. Encourage them to join in the worship until it is finished and then continue their visit afterwards. If they have limited time and must visit with their friend or relative, visitors will often move away from the service. Assist them in this if necessary so that there may be minimal disruption of the service.

PREPARING A MESSAGE

We offer here some suggestions to those who are not accustomed to delivering a Bible message as well as to those who might want to improve their skills:

1. Familiarize yourself with the Scripture passage on which you are going to base your message. Read and reread the passage in its larger context. Pray for insight to understand and present the passage faithfully. If possible, memorize the key text.
2. Pick several key words or concepts from the passage, and study them in light of the whole of Scripture. In studying Matthew 5:6, for example, look at the image of hungering and thirsting, as well as being satisfied, in both the Old and New Testaments. Also explore the concepts of blessedness and righteousness.
3. Summarize the main point of the passage in a simple sentence. It is important, especially with the elderly, to be both crystal clear and concise. Making such a summary will help you to do this. An example of such a sentence, using Matthew 5:6 as a base, would be: "In order to be righteous we must desire it with our whole being."
4. Prayerfully seek out applications of this passage to present daily situations in your life and the lives of the elderly. Reformulate your summary sentence with these applications in mind, using the word *you* so that your audience will be clear on what *they* can do differently in response to your preaching.
5. As you actually write the message, work backwards from your conclusion (i.e., the application). Ask yourself questions like what? where? how? and why? about the application, in order that all you say will point to your single conclusion.

Guidelines for Bible Messages

Relate to the Past

For many elderly people there are strong elements of the past that need to be appreciated, evaluated and often reconciled before God. There is a scriptural basis for this in Psalm 105. This psalm shows Israel in the process of reviewing and evaluating her past relationship with the Lord. You want to help the elderly—as the psalmist does in this psalm—to see the hand of God in their lives. Keep in mind general areas that are areas of difficulty for many older people, such as bitterness, anger, grief or guilt, and use them as themes for your message. People should be able to make personal application to their own lives.

Relate to the Present

Many people use reflection on the past not to resolve conflicts, but to escape present conditions. Seek to involve elderly people in the present. Remember their present afflictions such as loneliness, pain, feelings of uselessness, etc. Speak to these concerns specifically. In order to help them relate to the present speak to them of what God is doing today in the world, in the church and even in their own nursing home.

Relate to the Future

Convey the hope we have as Christians both in this life and the life to come. Emphasize the promises of God and his great faithfulness. The resurrection is central to our hope (see John 3:16b; Col. 3:1–4; 1 John 3:2, 3; Rev. 21, 22).

As you relate your messages to the past, present and future, keep in mind the following general suggestions:

1. Exhort your congregation to faith, to hope, to love and to service of God *now* (see 2 Corinthians 1 and any of the praise or lament psalms—e.g., 22, 77, 143, 113–118) for some scriptural support for this as well as the scriptural patterns.
2. Build many of your messages on a consistent theme. Emphasizing one theme over a long period is valuable, for it gives stability to their lives and helps make meaningful connections for them week by week. For instance, you might try a series of sermons on Psalm 23, the Lord's Prayer or the Sermon on the Mount. Whatever theme you choose to unite your messages, be sure it is applicable to the nursing home situation.
3. Use vivid illustrations to clarify your main points. Make sure you use images that the elderly can relate to easily—e.g., holiday seasons, birthdays, weddings, family gatherings, relationships, nature, etc. Share illustrations from your own life also, as long as they are things the elderly can identify with.
4. Quote the old, familiar hymns in your sermons, as well as using them for singing. (Remember that what is familiar to *you* may not be familiar to them.)
5. State the gospel clearly somewhere in your message, and perhaps often. John 3:16 is a familiar verse that contains a central aspect of the gospel and fits nicely into many different messages.
6. Repeat, repeat, repeat. Repetition is very necessary in all teaching, especially in a nursing home. Repetition provides coherence to a talk and can clarify and communicate your main point. You may want to recite and possibly help the residents to memorize a certain text as part of your message.
7. Simplify your message to one or two main ideas. Elaborate, amplify, explain, illustrate, repeat and otherwise dwell upon and seek to communicate that main thrust. Use your hymns and prayers to reinforce this same point. The use of explicit biblical language is one good way to communicate simply. The message *must be kept short* (ten to fifteen minutes).

CONDUCTING BIBLE STUDIES

Conducting a study of Scripture in a nursing home can be very similar to conducting a worship service. Because of the short attention span of many older people, a lengthy exposition of a Scripture passage is not advisable. An inductive Bible study, in which questions are asked in order to bring out the main points, is often most helpful, especially when the residents are alert and verbally responsive. Otherwise, a short explanation is appropriate, with questions interspersed if possible. Remember that people may fall asleep if they are not actively participating.

Below is a format for a Bible study that incorporates a few elements of worship as well. Obviously this format can be abbreviated considerably if time or circumstances necessitate.

Prayer
Hymn(s)
Reading of Scripture
Study of Scripture (including questions and discussion)
Prayer—based on the study and its implications
Hymn

We have found the following passages to be excellent for verse-by-verse (and week-by-week) treatment. Dealing with only one verse at each study is good because a single verse is more easily remembered than a longer passage. And we do recommend encouraging the memorization of the verse as a part of the study. The continuous treatment of one text has seemed most wise. In this way a wide field of thought is covered in a unified way, but yet in "bite-sized" portions.

Suggested Passages:
1. Psalm 23
2. The Lord's Prayer
3. Matthew 5–7 (The Sermon on the Mount)
4. Selected topics and themes as appropriate

Bible study guides on selected passages and themes can also be adapted for use in nursing homes.

EVANGELISM

"Evangelism in the Nursing Home" is a topic about which there has been considerable discussion. There are many who believe our main purpose in visitation should be to befriend the elderly and help meet their physical and emotional needs, offering spiritual guidance only if it is requested. Others stress the priority of direct evangelism and desire to submit all other aims to this one overarching purpose. Elderly people are so near to death, this latter group claims, that we must constantly proclaim verbally the gospel and urge repentance, lest they also perish eternally.

Coming to terms with these two different opinions is no easy task. Granted, many people you visit are facing imminent death. This does not mean, however, that there is not *enough* time for the Holy Spirit to work. Overzealous evangelists who proclaim the gospel without first becoming acquainted with the person and accurately determining his needs can often do more harm than good. The good news of Jesus Christ is a gift and it must be offered as a gift, not used as a threat or a weapon.

On the other hand, sickness, an imminent operation, loneliness, grief or depression—all are deep spiritual needs that can be met by the gospel as it is offered even by someone hitherto unknown to the sufferer. We must be sensitive to the fact that God has perhaps prepared someone for us to share the gospel with and we must be ready to give the gift that has so freely been given to us.

There is no single answer as to when and how to evangelize. The key to discovering what to do in any given situation is the Holy Spirit. God has gone before us and we must respond to what he has already done and is continuing to do in people's hearts.

Our response at times may be simply showing God's love through our actions. Or we may have opportunity to share the gospel verbally. In either case, we must be people of prayer who are actively relying on God's guidance before, during and following our visits.

As we seek to be guided in our evangelism, we must not overlook the fact that God has given each of us different gifts. Some people are skilled in the "art of friendship." They can make a lasting impression of God's love and care simply through a long, committed friendship. Others have gifts for sharing the gospel directly with people whom they don't know. We must each evaluate God's gifts to us, making sure we are truly honest in our motivation. On the one hand, the "friend" must not hold back from sharing the good news of Christ for fear of being thought foolish. The "evangelist," on the other hand, should not avoid making friends for fear of becoming involved and committed.

With these initial thoughts in mind, the following suggestions should be considered:

1. A worship service for believers is evangelism for the unconverted. The simple, direct gospel (e.g., John 3:16ff.) shared throughout a service is an encouragement and comfort for believers and a call to faith for nonbelievers.
2. In individual visitation, in the context of an established, caring relationship, one good way to open conversation is to share some recent insight or activity of God in your life.
3. Literature provides another avenue for evangelism. Subordinate the literature to personal communication. Share from the literature before leaving it. Avoid, when possible, mass distribution of literature without personal contact.
4. Be sensitive to the needs of the individual you are visiting. These needs —often very near the surface—provide a wonderful opportunity to express the truth and compassion of Jesus Christ.
5. Sharing openly with a Christian resident in a room where there are non-Christians present can be another effective method of evangelism. We have found great interest among roommates when they see the joy and peace that a relationship with God through Christ can bring. Sometimes there may be only a desire to be noticed—but that, too, offers a chance to befriend and share more openly. Encourage Christian residents to share their faith with other residents who do not know Christ.
6. See "What Is Visitation?" (in Part III) for further information on how to share the gospel through using yourself, Scripture and prayer.
7. Evangelism with the elderly is in many respects like evangelism with any other person. Therefore, we recommend the reading and study of any good book on the topic of evangelism. We suggest the following books:

Ford, Leighton. *Good News Is for Sharing*. Elgin, Ill.: David C. Cook Pub. Co., 1977.

Little, Paul. *How to Give Away Your Faith*. Chicago: InterVarsity Press, 1966.

MacNair, Donald. *The Living Church*. Philadelphia: Great Commission Publications, 1980.

Metzger, Will. *Tell the Truth*. Downers Grove, Ill.: InterVarsity Press, 1981.

Miller, C. John. *Evangelism and Your Church*. Phillipsburg, N.J.: Presbyterian and Reformed Pub. Co., 1980.

Pippert, Rebecca Manley. *Out of the Salt Shaker: Evangelism as a Way of Life*. Downers Grove, Ill.: InterVarsity Press, 1980.

Rinker, Rosalyn, and Griffith, Harry. *Sharing God's Love*. Grand Rapids: Zondervan Pub. House, 1976.

Sammy, Lorne. *The Art of Personal Witnessing*. Chicago: Moody Press, 1957.

Spurgeon, Charles Haddon. *The Soul Winner or, How to Lead Sinners to the Savior*. London: Marshall, n.d.

Stott, John R. W. *Personal Evangelism*. London: InterVarsity Press, 1969.

Turnbull, Charles T. G. *Taking Men Alive*. London: Lutterworth Press, 1957.

PART V

ORGANIZING THE CHURCH FOR MINISTRY

While the major thrust of this manual is to help Christians in a nursing home ministry, this final part enlarges the scope a bit to help churches organize to meet the needs of elderly people both inside and outside of nursing homes.

This part is adapted from "Developing Programs for Senior Citizens—A Handbook for Churches," produced by the Delaware County (of Pa.) Services for the Aging, and is included here with their permission. We gratefully acknowledge the editors: Judy Oerkvitz, Louis Colbert, Norma Thomas and Verne Dalton.

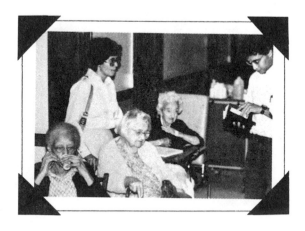

INTRODUCTION

Churches have historically sought to minister to the special needs of widows, orphans and the aged. Today many churches are reexamining their efforts along these lines in light of the changing cultural and social situation. As concern for the plight of the aged has increased, so too have the resources available to the church. Health systems, social agencies and informational services all stand ready to provide support to churches taking on new projects or otherwise strengthening their ministry with the aging.

The purpose of this section is threefold:

1. To provide general guidelines as to how a church can plan a program to serve and involve the older adult
2. To offer some suggestions about how to plan, organize and maintain an effective volunteer program
3. To suggest ideas for the kinds of programs that churches could undertake to help alleviate problems faced by senior citizens

This section has been designed to provide an overview of the major elements of program development. Detailed instruction has necessarily been omitted due to the fact that program development and implementation will vary according to the particular situation of a given church.

HOW TO PLAN YOUR PROGRAM

Develop a Planning Committee

Organize a committee responsible for looking into program ideas and developing a plan to extend the church's ministry to/with the aging. Ideally, this committee should consist of the pastor, one or more members of the church's governing body and several members of the congregation. It is recommended that older people themselves be recruited for this committee. The responsibility of the committee will be to survey the needs and resources, define the problems, develop plans for problem resolution, work to initiate programs, review the problems in light of program impact and make appropriate program adjustments.

Survey the Needs

Before a program can be developed, the church must have a clear idea of the unmet needs of elderly people in the church and surrounding community. It may be useful to develop a questionnaire which can be used in talking with elderly members of the church, relatives of church members and community residents. Statistics from the local municipality may be helpful. Interviews with local elected officials, staff from neighborhood health and welfare organizations and other health care delivery systems, and the area agency on aging should be able to help the planning committee discover the problem areas of elderly people in the community. Prioritize the unmet needs and service gaps.

Gather Suggestions for Programs

The sky is the limit when it comes to ideas for possible programs. Plan a way to involve as many of the congregation as possible in brainstorming ideas and discussing alternative approaches to the problems that have been uncovered. From this you should also be able to determine where people's interests lie, as well as generate enthusiasm.

Choose a Strategy

There are two basic strategies which might be used. The first is for the church to develop linkages with existing programs serving senior citizens, such as Meals on Wheels or the Retired Senior Volunteer Program. The church could recruit volunteers of all ages from within the congregation to help extend these services to additional elderly people. Older people who have unmet needs could be referred to these and other agencies for services.

The second strategy is to establish a new program, such as a Senior Club or Friendly Visiting Program, using the church as a base. This kind of approach will probably involve greater expenditures of time, personnel and resources, but might also bring greater satisfaction to all concerned. Programs can be a "one-shot" operation or an ongoing activity.

When deciding which approach to take, the planning committee will need

to consider the following factors:
1. What is the mission of the church? How would this program fit in?
2. What are the unmet needs of the elderly in the church and surrounding community?
3. What are the church's resources?
   a. What are the facilities of the church building (kitchen, lounge, gym, library)? Would a program conflict with other activities currently taking place in the church building? Is the church accessible by public transportation?
   b. What equipment and supplies are available (bus, mimeograph, tables, chairs, games)?
   c. What is the financial situation of the church? How would it be possible to raise funds needed for the program?
   d. Who belongs to the congregation? What skills and interests do they have? What groups within the church might be interested in working on a program for senior citizens? When are they available? Are there other groups that use church facilities which might want to become involved? (For example: Scout troops, community groups)

Draw Up a Plan

After considering these factors and deciding on an approach, the committee should draw up a plan for each specific program. The plan should include the following components:
1. Statement of the goal(s) of the program, and the specific objectives to be achieved during a target period. Objectives are specific ends to be reached and should be stated in a concrete way. (For example, an objective might read: To develop a volunteer shopping-assistance program to serve at least five older people each week . . .)
2. A discussion of how the program will be organized and implemented. Consider how many volunteers and/or staff members will be needed. For what tasks? Who will coordinate their efforts? How will it be done? What population will receive this service? By what means will they be recruited/invited/referred? What will the costs be, if any? What records will need to be kept, if any? To whom will the program be accountable? How will the senior citizens served be involved in the planning and decision-making processes?
3. A plan for evaluating the progress of the program. What will be the timetable for developing this program? How will you know if your goals and objectives have been met? Plan to review the program annually and to plan ahead for the future on a regular basis.

Plan a program to begin on a small scale but leave room for growth. Increase the size gradually as strengths and weaknesses become evident and as more people become interested. Once the plan has been written, solicit comments and suggestions from the entire congregation and modify the plan as needed to obtain majority support.

Implement the Plan

In order to implement the plan, it is helpful to develop a detailed list of the steps involved and a timetable specifying when they will be accomplished. Identify members of the congregation to be responsible for such steps as purchasing supplies and equipment, developing linkages with community resources, raising funds and recruiting volunteers. Make sure that somebody is responsible for coordinating this process.

It is important at this point to set up periodic check points for evaluating how the program is functioning. These periodic reviews will enable you to make modifications to the plan based on experience, to make sure that all aspects of the program are being implemented in proper sequence and to make sure that the plan is accomplishing what it has set out to do.

HOW TO GET A VOLUNTEER PROGRAM STARTED . . .
AND KEEP IT GOING

Coordination and Supervision

For any program, someone must take responsibility for delegating tasks, coordinating activities, keeping records and accounts, etc. Depending on the program, these functions may be handled by a small committee or a single individual, by volunteers or paid staff. Supervision is also a crucial function in volunteer programs. Each group of six to twelve volunteers should be supervised by a person who can provide ongoing support, recognize the need for further training and help when troubles arise.

Recruiting Volunteers

Volunteers can be recruited through announcements in newsletters and newspapers, via notices on bulletin boards and through personal contacts. When a person is asked to volunteer, he or she should be told what tasks are involved, approximately how much time they will take and what benefits will be provided to the volunteer him/herself. An effort should be made to allow each volunteer some choice of activities and to tailor tasks to meet the individual's skills and interests.

Some thought should be given to the circumstances of potential volunteers. Are they mostly mothers with young children at home? Maybe more volunteers would be forthcoming if a babysitting program were set up to care for their children while they work on the program. If the volunteers are elderly, they may need transportation to enable them to become involved. If youth groups are involved, activities will need to be scheduled in the late afternoon and early evening hours.

Volunteer Training

Once a volunteer pool has been established, training should be provided. Be sure to include a discussion of issues relating to aging, an orientation to the overall program being offered, information about specific tasks which volunteers will be doing and notice of problems which may arise and how to handle them. It is useful to do some roleplaying so that volunteers can participate in simulated situations similar to those they may actually encounter. Each volunteer should receive a written description of what he/she is expected to do, and a contact person should be designated for future reference. A volunteer contract can be a useful tool for specifying basic standards of performance and lines of accountability.

It should be expected that a certain percentage of volunteers will drop out of the program shortly after it starts. There are many reasons for this: a change in one's personal situation which makes volunteering inconvenient, a misunderstanding of what is required, or anxiety about one's performance. Plan to follow up with all new volunteers, particularly those whose enthusiasm seems to be lagging. Sometimes a bit of personal support is all that is needed. In other cases the volunteer may be more comfortable if he/she is assigned to a different task.

Ongoing Support for Volunteers

After a person has begun work as a volunteer, he or she cannot be forgotten or taken for granted. Continuing supervision and support are needed to deal with problems and questions as they arise, to help maintain the individual's enthusiasm, and to give the volunteer recognition for the valuable work he/she is doing.

Support activities might include a monthly meeting for all Friendly Visitors to share their feelings and experiences, an in-service training session for drivers to teach safe-driving tips for winter road conditions, or a friendly phone call from the supervisor to each volunteer to help keep things running smoothly and answer questions. Be sure to plan these support and in-service training sessions for times which are convenient and provide transportation, babysitting or other services as needed. Remember to evaluate volunteers regularly to make sure that they are living up to the standards of their contract.

New volunteers will probably need to be recruited and trained periodically. Take steps to help them become integrated with the "old" volunteers.

Volunteer Recognition

Very few people will do something for nothing. Although most volunteers will derive a sense of personal satisfaction from their work, a volunteer recognition program is important in keeping them going. Besides personal feedback, volunteers can be recognized through newsletter and newspaper articles, bulletin board displays, special luncheons and dinners, and community or church programs. Use photographs and awards to recognize one or two individuals each month. An annual recognition event is often scheduled. Praise people for work well done, but above all be sincere.

IDEAS FOR PROGRAMS

Spotlight on the Church Itself

Before a church contemplates starting new service projects to help the aging, it might be advisable to look at how well existing church programs are serving the elderly and to explore ways to increase the involvement of senior citizens in church affairs. In this section, we suggest a number of questions to help a church conduct a self-evaluation and some ideas for improvement:

1. Do older members of the church attend services and activities regularly? If not, why not? Do they lack transportation that could be provided by other church members?
2. How are older members of the church made to feel wanted? Are they encouraged to serve on church boards and committees?
3. Do church activities appear to be age-segregated? Is this desirable? How can you help church members of all ages interact with one another in a meaningful way?
4. Is the church accessible to older people, especially those with disabilities? Can the building be entered without climbing steps? Perhaps a ramp could be built. Are bathroom facilities accessible? Perhaps support bars could be installed.
5. Could someone with a hearing defect hear the pastor deliver the sermon? Maybe it would be helpful to install a public address system, or headphones in one or more pews. Could a person with failing eyesight read the prayer book or hymnal? If large-print editions are not available, this might become a project for the congregation.
6. Are topics of interest to the elderly included in church programming? Maybe the church could sponsor an educational seminar on how to write a will and invite an attorney in to assist individuals. How about a discussion series on planning for retirement? A program explaining how to make funeral arrangements might include a chance for parents and adult children to discuss these important plans with one another.
7. Old age is a time of losses: physical, mental, personal and social. Clergy members have traditionally been, and continue to be, an important source of counseling and support for older people. New techniques such as "life review" may help a minister to extend his counseling skills. Workshops and courses on death and dying may enable a minister to better understand the mourning process and thus provide more support to members of the congregation.

Every church has important resources to offer to older adults, but sometimes nobody knows about them. If you think this might be the case in your situation, you could increase the visibility of the church's ministry to the aging by including a special column in the church newsletter, submitting articles to local newspapers and giving special recognition to senior citizens in church announcements.

Friendly Visiting Program

A Friendly Visiting Program is a way of arranging regular visits between a volunteer and an older person, in his or her home. The objectives of the program are to relieve loneliness; to bring friendship, interests and reasonable activities to the elderly; and to assist them in utilizing community resources. A Friendly Visitor makes a commitment to be a friend on a long-term basis, and usually visits once a week or every other week. An active senior citizen can become a Friendly Visitor for a less mobile person.

To arrange a Friendly Visiting Program, you will need: a supervisor or coordinator, a group of older people who desire to have Friendly Visitors and a group of volunteer visitors.

The supervisor is responsible for training, matching clients with Visitors, preparing the Visitor by sharing important information about the client, accompanying the Visitor on the initial visit, and providing follow-up support to the Visitor. This person will need to devote several hours or days each week. Although much of the coordination can be done by telephone, the supervisor will probably need to have personal transportation readily available. The supervisor is also responsible for arranging support activities such as a monthly meeting for all Friendly Visitors, further training and volunteer recognition.

A group of clients can be developed by the church in coordination with local social service agencies. As a result of outreach efforts, the church may learn of older people who would like to have a Friendly Visitor. Social service agencies may also locate potential clients and refer them to this program. An alternative approach is to arrange a Friendly Visiting Program between the church and a nearby nursing home or institution for the elderly.

The Friendly Visitors volunteer an hour or two each week. When visiting their friends, they may spend time talking, reading, assisting with letter writing, playing games, etc. The Friendly Visitor is also expected to report situations of stress or need to his or her supervisor so that a referral can be made to obtain needed help. Friendly Visitors will need to have transportation or to walk to their friend's home.

A Friendly Visiting Program involves only a moderate amount of time, coordination and money, yet it can bring a great deal of happiness both to older people and to volunteers. It is in harmony with the humanitarian principles of all religious groups and fits easily into most people's weekly schedules. For this reason, it is an ideal way for a church to extend its ministry to the aging.

Telephone Reassurance Program
A Telephone Reassurance Program is also a way of linking volunteers with older adults to relieve loneliness and to develop friendships. In addition, a Telephone Reassurance Program is a way of checking on the health and safety of older adults who live alone.

To arrange a Telephone Reassurance Program, you will also need a supervisor, a client group and a group of volunteer callers who will make a commitment to be a friend on a long-term basis. The roles of the supervisor and client group are similar to those described for the Friendly Visiting Program.

The caller volunteers to telephone his or her partner daily on the basis of a prearranged schedule. The daily conversation need not be long, although it is expected that as the individuals become friends, they will have more to talk about and may want to visit one another occasionally. If the older adult does not answer the telephone, however, the caller will take steps to make sure that the older adult is all right. The caller will follow a specified procedure developed by the Telephone Reassurance Program. (This might include calling the person every fifteen minutes for the next hour and—if the phone remains unanswered—calling a neighbor, the police or fire rescue squad to investigate.) In this way, the older adult is reassured by knowing that if he or she should become hurt or ill, and unable to call for assistance, he or she will be discovered and cared for within a reasonable period of time.

Like Friendly Visiting, a Telephone Reassurance Program does not involve complicated equipment or a great amount of time, but it is a small way to bring peace of mind to older people.

Personal Assistance Program
A Personal Assistance Program for older people is simply what it says: a way of arranging for volunteers to help older people with difficult tasks, either on a regular basis or once in a while.

Some examples of assistance that might be provided are:
  Someone to help an older person with failing eyesight write checks, pay bills and go to the bank, once or twice a month.
  Someone to offer shopping assistance to an older person once a week.
  Someone to prepare meals and assist in personal hygiene for a few days if an older person becomes ill.
  Someone to assist an older person in occasional heavy cleaning, such as spring-cleaning the attic, garage or cellar.
  Someone to rake leaves in the fall.
  Someone to cut grass once a week during the spring and summer.
  Someone to fix a broken appliance and do other minor repairs.
  Someone to assist in light cleaning on a regular basis, once a week.

To arrange a Personal Assistance Program requires the following:
1. Detective work, to find out what needs to be done and to offer helpful assistance to older people who might be reticent about asking.
2. Some imagination in recruiting volunteers for each task. Maybe a Scout troop that meets in the church could do yard maintenance over the summer or a youth group could do spring-cleaning for several individuals. A retired man might be happy to provide Handy-Andy assis-

tance to several older women. An older woman might be happy to use her cooking skills to help another in need. Think about all the people and groups affiliated with the church and attempt to involve as many as possible.

3. A coordinator, responsible for matching requests for assistance with volunteers willing and able to provide it.
4. Publicity to make the service known to all church and community members. It might be helpful to publicize a phone number in the church newsletter and local newspapers and to remind church members whenever announcements are made.

Remember to update the files of volunteers periodically, as people's skills and availability may change over a period of time.

Although a Personal Assistance Program might begin as a way of helping older people, it might end up as a Talent Exchange involving all members of the church in helping *one another*, using older persons as both clients and resource people.

Adopt-A-Grandparent

An Adopt-A-Grandparent Program is based on the idea that younger people and older people need one another, and that each role in a traditional family system (children, parents, grandparents) is important for the growth and development of other family members. In modern society, many families live in different parts of the country, too far to interact with one another on a regular basis. In other families, significant family members have died, leaving gaps in the family system. Under an Adopt-A-Grandparent Program, younger families and older adults are matched up with one another and establish a relationship similar to that between grandparents and natural families. Such a relationship might include interaction including frequent telephone contacts and visits, shared holiday and birthday celebrations, and a pattern of reciprocal services that family members perform for one another (e.g., transportation, child care, cooking, home repairs, etc.).

To set up an Adopt-A- Grandparent Program, the following steps need to be taken:

1. Identify older adults and younger families who wish to participate in the program.
2. Match them up and arrange for them to meet one another. Make sure that people are compatible and share significant interests and values. Make sure both have a chance to decide whether or not they wish to "adopt" each other.
3. Assist them in developing a mutually satisfying relationship. Remember that not all older adults have been parents or natural grandparents. Some churches have assisted older adults in becoming grandparents by sponsoring a series of discussions about "how to be a creative grandparent," and offering suggestions for ways to relate to young children.

It might also be possible to institute an Adopt-A-Grandparent relationship with older people in a nursing home or extended care facility. Be sure to discuss the nature of the program with the administrator and work out details of transportation, meals, visiting, etc. Both families and potential grandparents must share common expectations for the program.

Although we have discussed Adopt-A-Grandparent as a formally established program, we must point out that this kind of "adoption" often occurs naturally when older adults and younger people come to know each other through participation in other kinds of programs, such as Friendly Visiting or through informal interaction within the framework of a common church or neighborhood.

Adopt-A-Home

Nursing homes, institutions for the aging, and long-term care facilities are all institutions out of the mainstream of thought and activity of the regular community. Because the residents of these facilities are unable to get out to participate in normal activities, many suffer from enforced social and cultural isolation.

Life does not have to be this way. We have the option of bringing the outside world in through cooperation between a church and an institution. This type of commitment should be a long-term commitment, not just a seasonal one, although special seasonal activities are always appropriate.

The nature, style and frequency of involvement of a church with a nursing home or extended care facility would vary according to the particular needs of the facility and the resources of the providers. Programs could vary from a monthly sing-along provided by church choir and organist, to an arts and crafts program, to a church-sponsored picnic for residents, to an ongoing Friendly Visiting Program for individual residents.

Programs should be set up well in advance with the facility administrator. Consistency of commitment is a key ingredient to program success.

Guardianship

If an older person becomes mentally incompetent, unable to handle his or her day-to-day affairs, and seems to have no family or relatives available to make decisions for his care, he may be in need of a legally established guardian.

There are two forms of guardianship. A "Guardian of the Person" is an individual responsible for making decisions regarding the personal well-being of another: e.g., where the person will live, whether he should be institutionalized, etc. A "Guardian of the Estate" is an individual responsible for making decisions regarding the estate and financial situation of another to further that person's well-being. Because a guardian of the estate can receive a certain percentage of the estate in return for providing management, it is often possible to arrange for a bank, lawyer or insurance firm to take on this responsibility, if there are significant assets involved. However, many older people have little more than a few pieces of furniture and their monthly social security check, and it is very difficult to find persons willing to take on responsibility for managing these assets. It is possible for one person to assume guardianship of both the person and the estate.

There is a great need for caring, responsible adults to serve as guardians for older people no longer able to make decisions for themselves. Members of your church might be competent and willing to assume this role. To be a guardian, one must accept a permanent relationship of responsibility for another; one must keep accurate records of financial and interpersonal transactions; one must be able to weigh the needs of the other when making decisions; and one must be accountable to the court. The guardian thus functions as both advocate and caretaker.

Transportation Assistance Program
A Transportation Assistance Program is another means of linking volunteers with older adults to provide a variety of transportation services, such as trips to doctors, hospitals, therapists, churches, stores, friends, etc. To establish a Transportation Assistance Program you will need a coordinator, a client group and volunteer drivers with cars.

The program can operate several ways, depending on the coordinator's style, the needs of the client group and the number of volunteers. A system to request rides several days in advance usually works well, with provisions for a small number of emergency trips. Coordinators can arrange trips according to days people want to go or according to geographic locations desired. Generally, volunteers drive persons closest to their homes. No-fault insurance, as required by law, covers both passengers and drivers in case of accidents.

Volunteers would register with the coordinator, specifying the day and/or days they wish to volunteer and the hours each day. Older adults needing transportation would call a predetermined number to make reservations in advance. The coordinator would then match a volunteer with a client and confirm reservations with both parties.

Churches that wish to provide transportation specifically for Sunday services can develop a program similar to car pooling. You would need someone to coordinate this activity. Persons attending services regularly who have additional space in their cars would be potential volunteers. Volunteers would register with the coordinator along with older persons desiring transportation to church. The coordinator would then match volunteers with riders according to geographic locations. Of course, the coordinator would have to set up procedures to follow when one of the two parties cannot make it.

A Transportation Assistance Program can be a tremendous asset to your community; it can provide a means to keep people happy and productive during their later years.

Senior Citizen Clubs

A Senior Citizen Club is a group of people who get together to perform some tasks and/or for social-emotional reasons. In most cases, these clubs' first function is to provide a setting for interaction, social supports and just plain fun. It is important to note that both locally and nationally it has been found that Senior Groups can be an effective means of preventing and resolving isolation and its attendant problems. In addition to providing a place for social contacts and friendships, it functions in a variety of other ways. These clubs also provide a way for re-involving the elderly in society, demonstrating and developing skills and talents of older people, providing a locus for advocacy and linking older people in need with services.

A church that is concerned about the associational needs of its senior citizens should examine these clubs to determine whether the church could support or revitalize an existing club or whether it would be appropriate to establish a church-sponsored group. It is likely that some people would be inclined to join a club simply because it is church-related. On the other hand, of course, if a club is too closely associated with its church sponsor, it might hamper an open membership policy.

The following steps are appropriate in order to establish a Senior Club:
1. Determine the number of older adults in your congregation and community and examine their needs. Is there a need for a Senior Citizen Club?
2. Form a steering committee of senior citizens —
   To provide the initial leadership
   To educate the group
   To recruit members
   To set up the initial meeting
3. Set up an initial club meeting.
   Choose an appropriate and convenient setting.
   Set up the agenda to include a speaker or film or other event of general interest.
   Plan for the election of officers (at least temporary ones).
   Allow for a general discussion on the direction of the club for the future.
   Include a time for socialization. Refreshments and name tags help people feel comfortable with a new group of people.
   When setting up an initial meeting one should remember that a luncheon is an extremely good way of getting people to turn out. People are generally willing to pay for this. However, a luncheon meeting will take more planning, even if it is catered. To get an accurate meal count, reservations need to be taken in advance.

4. Recruit participants.

   A public relations officer could be appointed from the steering committee to see that local papers carry advance notice of the meeting. Invitations will need to be sent out. Personal contacts and phone contacts are the most effective way to get people to commit themselves. It may take several meetings before a core group of interested persons is developed to form the nucleus of a club.

5. Provide transportation or make arrangements for car pooling. Attentention should be given to transportation and escort services. Some people do not like to arrive alone. Others may be unable to participate unless they have transportation provided.

6. Assist in club and program development.

   After the club is established it may be necessary to provide continued support to assist in the institution of a permanent structure, developing volunteer or staff skills and the establishing of a sound financial base.

Rotating Fund

It is inevitable, given our busy pace of life, that not all members of a church will be willing or able to volunteer time to extend the church's ministry to the aging. However, there may be some individuals who are willing to contribute funds, others who will work on fund-raising projects. These funds may be used to support programs described above by paying for salaries, rent, equipment or volunteer expenses; or they may be combined to form a *Rotating Fund* to meet special needs of elderly citizens. Here are some ideas for how the money could be used:

> To install a telephone and pay the monthly bills for a senior citizen to allow him or her to participate in the Telephone Reassurance Program.
>
> To extend low-interest loans to older people for home repairs.
>
> To assist older people in paying fuel bills incurred during extremely cold winters.
>
> To assist an older person in paying for dialysis needed on a regular basis.
>
> To build a ramp or install a chair lift for a person who becomes disabled (to allow him or her to continue living at home).
>
> To provide glasses, a hearing aid or dentures for a needy person.
>
> To stock an emergency food closet.

A THEOLOGICAL POSTSCRIPT:

Old Folks at Home

by Mike Preg

Up to this point we have been considering ways to minister to elderly persons who reside in nursing homes. In this brief postscript we have an opportunity to reflect on the larger issue of whether Christians ought to allow nursing homes to take away the responsibilities of families. The author is a pastor in the Presbyterian Church in America.

∗ ∗ ∗ ∗

In her nonfiction book *The Summer of Great-grandmother,* Madeleine L'Engle describes the problems, crises, frustrations and guilt engendered by her mother's rapid slide into senility. Reflecting on her mother's situation vis-a-vis that of her earlier ancestors, she captures the frustrations and sympathies of each of us as we contemplate the encroachment of old age upon our own mothers and fathers.

> I look at Mother huddled in her chair by the window and think once more about Mado and Greatie. In a day of what we would consider primitive medical knowledge, and no hospitals as we understand hospitals today, they both lived to a ripe old age, with their wits about them. Up until Grandfather, there is no record of senility in the family. . . . Obviously, nursing homes have not caused senility in the elderly; but when grandmother or great-grandmother continued to live with the larger family, to be given meaning because she could at least stir the soup or rock the baby, the climate for growing old and dying was more healthy than it is today. I cannot reproduce that climate for Mother. Surgery kept her alive at eighty-seven; antibiotics pulled her through pneumonia at eighty-eight. For what? For this?[1]

The number of aged and elderly persons is increasing as longevity increases. Residences and care for the aged through nursing and retirement homes is a large and growing enterprise in our country. In spite of their high cost and debilitating effect, these institutions have become the commonplace and accepted approaches to this "problem" in our culture. Many Christians are adopting this institutional approach with apparently little ethical reflection on the goals, motives and standards for care of the elderly. It is the thesis of this paper that the normal place of residence and care for the aged people of God should be in the households of their children. This thesis will be examined from the situational, motivational and normative perspectives.

The Situation

The aging process presents us with many difficulties, as individuals and as a society. As individuals, the fear of death is removed in Christ, but advances in medical technology have made it possible for us to outlive our capacity to cope with sickness. For many persons, there is the threat of long-term illness at the end of life which will both wipe out their financial resources and leave the person hanging—seemingly indefinitely—between life and death.[2] As a society, the problem of aging has us caught between the twin jaws of rampant escalation in the costs for caring for the elderly and the projected increase in our elderly population—which is expected to double to 52 million over the next 50 years.[3]

Therefore, in spite of the technologically advanced state of our society, old age is the source of frustration and futility. It is surely a fact that in Adam our bodies along with the rest of creation were subjected to frustration by God (Rom. 8:20; cf. Gen. 3:19). In fact, our physical bodies are a focus of that futility and the redemption of the whole creation is particularly linked to the redemption of the bodies of the sons of God (Rom. 8:19–23). This frustration can not and will not be overcome by the technological advances of man. Gerontology[4] and geriatrics[5] are two of our fastest-growing fields of scientific endeavor and while they certainly will continue to alleviate human suffering, the ultimate frustration of the curse of God upon the sin of man will be with us until the end of the age. Gerontologists would do well to study the remarkably accurate description of old age in the twelfth chapter of Ecclesiastes. Even amid the softening effect of the humorous metaphors, we cannot help being struck by the stark reality with which the Preacher begins his description as he speaks of the "evil days" and the years when you will say, "I have no delight in them" (Eccl. 12:1). The Preacher feels and expresses the same frustration we feel as he cries out in verse 8, "All is vanity!" Here again, the connection between old age and the curse of Adam's race is made as verse 7 echoes the words of God (see Gen. 3:19) to our first ancestor, "Then the dust will return to the earth."

Yet, while the situation concerning the problem of old age is bleak as far as man is concerned, God has provided a solution in Jesus Christ, who alone can set us free from this body of death (Rom. 7:24). God graciously extends salvation to both the young and the old as he did when he brought Israel "with our young and our old" out of Egypt (Ex. 10:9). God has heard the plea of Psalm 71, "Do not cast me off in the time of old age" (vs. 9). The old are given a special place in the Messianic Kingdom: "Your old men shall dream dreams" (Joel 2:28; Acts 2:17) and "old men and old women will again sit in the streets of Jerusalem" (Zech. 8:4). These prophecies are typologically fulfilled in history as we see old men present when the restoration temple foundation is laid (Ezra 3:12). While the ultimate removal of the curse of old age must await the consummation, i.e., "the redemption of our body" (Rom. 8:23), nevertheless, as Christians we can understand that we have been subjected to futility, "in hope that the creation itself also will be set free from its slavery to corruption" (Rom. 8:20, 21). The believer who is united to Christ does not lose heart when he sees the decay of his outer man or physical body because by God's grace his inner man is being renewed day by day (2 Cor. 4:16). In fact, this decay of our bodies would appear to increase our attention toward and faith in eternal things as opposed to temporal things (2 Cor. 4:18). Seen in the light of redemption in Jesus Christ, the aging process functions in the life of the believer to wean him away from the temporal, the spurious values of life; and the aging process will be ultimately and finally arrested for eternity in the resurrection.[6]

From the situational perspective, there is yet another area which we need to investigate which bears more pointedly upon our thesis. Regardless of the important perspective gained from seeing old age in the light of the Fall and redemption in Christ, the fact remains that old people still require care above and beyond that which we would term medical care. The overwhelming approach of our society to provide this care has been and increasingly continues to be in the form of institutions.

> Only 5% of our older persons reside in institutions but this figure is misleading; the small percentage accounts for well over one million persons and one fourth of all persons over age 75 will enter nursing homes at some time in their lives. This figure will rise if alternatives are not created or improved.[7]

This situation darkens, however, when we take a look at the state of the institutions which offer care for the elderly:

> Nursing homes have been viewed as "the worst institution ever devised by man," and a U.S. Senate Report in December of 1974 concluded that a majority of this country's 23,000 nursing homes are substandard, with life-threatening violations of state and federal law.[8]

Anyone who regularly visits the elderly in nursing homes, as this writer has done over the past four years, can only have sympathy for this quoted assessment. Given this present situation, however, should we work to improve the institutions or must we ask the more basic question, Are they really necessary? Facilities which offer medical care to the aged, or to any age for that matter, can hardly be eliminated. Should custodial, nonmedical care of the aged properly be carried out in institutions?

> Studies carried out by gerontologists in the last several years are even more disturbing. As many as 40% of the elderly in nursing homes *do not* really need to be there . . . Many of those now in institutions would probably be maintained at home with minimal assistance . . .[9]

When we are looking at the care of the elderly people of God, theologically speaking we are in the area of the application of redemption. The church is certainly an important institution in carrying out the application of redemption. Throughout redemptive history, the people of God have been given the responsibility to care for the poor and the infirm. Widows are especially singled out, along with orphans, as special objects of the care and concern of the people of God (e.g., Deut. 14:29; Jas. 1:27). Jesus tells his sheep that it is their special privilege to care for "the least of them" (Matt. 25:40). The dependent status of the elderly in the midst of a society whose basic interest is profit has certainly tended to make them "least" in the eyes of many.[10]

Clearly, then, Christians are confronted with a responsibility to the elderly. In the area of the application of redemption, the question is often one of means—how is this responsibility to care for the elderly to be carried out? Throughout her history, the church has been in the business of old folks' homes.

However, as we look at the primary means through which God is pleased to apply redemption to his people, we see that the focus of the application of redemption is more fundamentally upon the family. The means by which God applies redemption in Christ to his people is through the Covenant of Redemption. God does not covenant with Abraham as an individual but with "you and your descendants after you" (Gen. 17:7). The eternality of God's covenant is expressed by "a thousand generations" (Deut. 7:9; Ps. 105:8–10). Presbyterians have always argued from these passages and their extension into the New Testament (Acts 2:39; Gal. 3:13ff.) as support for the inclusion of infants in the covenant community. Yet the solidarity of the family, a creation ordinance not abrogated by the Fall or redemption, has implications not only for the care and training of our children, but also for the care of our parents. Scripture gives several examples of this covenantal care of children *for* their parents.

In the midst of a famine in the land, Joseph said to his father, "And you shall live in the land of Goshen, and *you shall be near me*. . . . There I will also provide for you . . ." (Gen. 45:10, 11, italics added). Ruth left Moab and her people in order to care for her mother-in-law, Naomi (Ruth 1:15–17). In particular support of our thesis are Ruth's words to Naomi, ". . . where you go, I will go, and where you lodge, I will lodge" (vs. 16). Even after her marriage to Boaz, we conclude that Naomi went to live with Ruth and Boaz, serving as the nurse of young Obed (4:13–17). Lack of the presence of the older generation "in your *house*" is seen to be a curse upon Eli (1 Sam. 2:31, 32, italics added). Many implications have been drawn from Jesus' concern for his mother, Mary, while he was dying on the cross (John 19:26, 27), but certainly his provision for her serves as the preeminent example of this covenantal care and concern. Again it is significant that the NASB correctly renders the sense of the Greek in relating the response of the disciple whom Jesus loved as he "took her into his own household" (John 19:27). Timothy's sincere faith (2 Tim. 1:5) and knowledge of the Scriptures

(2 Tim. 3:15) would appear to be a product of an extended covenantal family consisting of at least his grandmother Lois and his mother Eunice (2 Tim. 1:5).

The Motivational Perspective

The difficulties involved in caring for elderly parents in the midst of our modern homes are legion. To begin with, most of today's homes are not large enough to provide separate apartment-type quarters to an aged parent. However, when the cost of institutional care is considered, the construction of an addition to our home becomes an attractive financial alternative. Most healthy middle-aged adults are physically able to handle the work involved in caring for an aged parent. Emotionally, however, things are somewhat more difficult as a recent study of relationships between the elderly and their adult children indicates.

> . . . poor health can increase the elderly parent's dependency on the adult child with an increase in resentment by the adult child (often caught between caring for his/her own children and caring for the elderly parent), and increasing frustration of the parent, with an over-all poorer relationship between parent and the child as the result.[11]

There is no question but that caring for an elderly parent in the home makes an imposition on the entire family and in the face of this difficulty, the motivation for doing so must be particularly strong. There is substantial opinion[12] that the onset of senility or the depression wrongly diagnosed as senility is caused by institutionalization and therefore should be significantly stayed by living as a part of a caring covenantal family. Nevertheless, increasing deterioration in health, forgetfulness, incontinence, immature behavior and bitterness are often the elderly parents' reaction to the care provided by their children. This rejection is perhaps the most difficult to deal with. Constant care is required and the elderly are simply not the cute, cuddly infants who make similar outrageous demands upon our time. In lieu of the day care centers for the elderly being proposed in our society, church members or other family members should volunteer regularly to temporarily care for elderly parents so that their children can have a few free days per week.

The burdens involved in caring for aged parents in our homes are heavy, indeed, but the motivation for doing so is even stronger. John Murray writes of our adoption as sons of God as the "highest and most intimate of relationships."[13] It is certainly this wonder of God's amazing grace that causes the apostle John to exclaim, "See how great a love the Father has bestowed upon us, that we should be called children of God" (1 John 3:1). John underlines our *present* status as children of God as he goes on to add, "and such we are" (cf. vs. 2). Murray calls this act of transfer from an alien family into the family of God himself "the apex of grace and privilege."[14] We now have boldness through the Spirit to address God as Father (Gal. 4:6; cf. Rom. 8:15, 16) and we are assured of the persistence of good gifts from our Father who is in heaven (Luke 11:11–13). This indicative status which we enjoy with respect to our heavenly Father is the gracious ground for our earthly sonship. In his infinite love God has given us, the former sons of disobedience (Eph. 2:2), the right (authority) to become children of God (John 1:12) and it is this particular love which constrains and motivates us to respond with filial love or covenant loyalty.

But our filial response to our heavenly Father is also to be directed toward our earthly mothers and fathers (Ex. 20:12; Eph. 6:1-3; Col. 3:20). We realize our adoption as sons of God by faith in Christ (John 1:12; Gal. 3:26) and James points out that our faith without works is dead (Jas. 2:26). Clearly, our faith in our adoption as sons of God works itself out in our proper filial relationship to our earthly parents. This is but a specific instance of our loving because he first loved us (1 John 4:11, 12), of faith working through love (Gal. 5:6) and the outworking of our salvation (Phil. 2;12, 13). Showing love to the unlovable, those who do not appreciate us, our enemies, is the mark of those who show themselves to be sons of their Father who is in heaven (Matt. 5:45; cf. Luke 6:35). Sonship is the consummate expression of the blessing of the covenant relationship between God and his people: "He who overcomes shall inherit these things, and I will be his God and he will be My son" (Rev. 21:7); and this is the supreme motivation for us to rejoice in the privilege of caring for our elderly parents in the midst of our extended covenantal family.

The Normative Perspective

Obviously one of our basic considerations is the fifth commandment, "Honor your father and mother." As we have already seen, there is a continuity between honoring parents and honoring God (Eph. 6:1; Col. 3:20).

Given this clear scriptural imperative to "honor" our parents and more generally, the aged, we must ask whether institutionalization is an obedient covenantal response. The following quotations from our government and social scientists would seem to say an emphatic no!

> Institutionalization can be very destructive for many of the elderly; the very process of becoming institutionalized, living in such a total environment, can be rather dehumanizing under the best of circumstances.[15]

> The care given in most nursing homes and homes for the aged is limited primarily to nursing and custodial care with no restorative or rehabilitation service. As a result, the great majority of the people in these homes deteriorate physically and mentally to the point of total disability.[16]

At one time most people assumed that the chief mental disorders in old age resulted purely from the inevitable breakdown of the person as an organism. Today, in contrast, the growing belief is that the kind of social relations experienced by the aged, such as isolation, and loss of status, help greatly to produce the disorders.[17]

... No longer are we under the mistaken notion that senility is something that "just happens" to older people. Much of it is caused by the emotional repercussions of an empty and forsaken existence. At this stage of life people simply cannot take the despair in being set aside .... forsakenness that these people experience from others can be projected also to God. In fact, they may also feel forsaken by the church, which makes the projection to God that much more logical...[18]

The implications are clear. The elderly in our churches and our own elderly parents are crying out like the psalmist to God, "Do not cast me off in the time of old age ... "(Ps. 71:9). As sons of God, and their sons and daughters, we must answer their cry—honoring them, supporting them, lifting them up and delivering them—by the simple act of graciously extending the bounds of our twentieth-century nuclear family to include our aged parents as members of our extended covenantal household. Institutionalization, except for definite medical reasons, would seem to be the twentieth-century equivalent of "casting off" or "forsaking."

Footnotes

1. Madeleine L 'Engle, *The Summer of Great-grandmother* (New York: Farrar, Straus and Giroux, 1974), p. 194.

2. "The Graying of America," *Newsweek,* 28 February 1977, p. 56.

3. Ibid., p. 50.

4. Gerontology: the biological science which deals with the aging process of life.

5. Geriatrics: the medical specialty of gerontology which studies and treats changes and diseases of the aging human system.

6. W. E. Hulme, *The Pastoral Care of Families, Its Theology and Practice* (New York: Abingdon Press, 1962), pp. 175-177.

7. Liz Karnes, *Alternatives to Institutionalization for the Aged: An Overview and Bibliography,* CPL Exchange Bibliography #877 (Monticello, Ill.: Council of Planning Librarians, Sept. 1975), p. 2.

8. Ibid., p. 1.

9. Ibid., p. 2.

10. H.J.M. Nouwen, "Aging and Ministry," *Journal of Pastoral Care,* 28 (1974), p. 166.

11. E. S. Johnson and B. J. Bursk, "Relationships Between the Elderly and Their Adult Children," *The Gerontologist,* 17, No. 1 (Feb. 1977), p. 96.

12. See, for instance: Hulme, p. 171 and Karnes, p. 2.

13. John Murray, *Redemption Accomplished and Applied* (Grand Rapids: Eerdmans, 1973), p. 139.

14. Ibid., p. 134.

15. Karnes, p. 2.

16. *Rehabilitation and Aging: A Statement of Rehabilitation Needs, Resources and Programs to-*

gether with Recommendations from the 1961 White House Conference on Aging, Series 11 (Washington, D.C.: Special Staff on Aging, US Department of Health, Education and Welfare, June 1961), p. 19.

17. Milton L. Barron, *The Aging American: An Introduction to Social Gerontology and Geriatrics* (New York: Thomas Y. Crowell Co., 1961), p. 50.

18. Hulme, p. 171.

List of Works Consulted

Barron, Milton L. *The Aging American: An Introduction to Social Gerontology and Geriatrics.* New York: Thomas Y. Crowell Co., 1961.

Calvin, John. *Institutes of the Christian Religion.* Trans. Henry Beveridge, Vol. I, Book II, pp. 344-346.

Chalmers, George. "Geriatric Medicine." *Medicine and the Christian Mind.* Ed. J. A. Vale. London: Christian Medical Fellowship, 1975.

Cross, Dennis W. "How Not to Retire on $400 a Month." *Aide, The Insurance Magazine from USAA.* Spring 1977, pp.18-20.

Dudley, C. J. and Hillery, G. A. "Freedom and Alienation in Homes for the Aged." *The Gerontologist.* Vol. 17, No. 2, April 1977, p. 144.

Hendriksen, William. *New Testament Commentary: Exposition of the Pastoral Epistles.* Grand Rapids: Baker Book House, 1957.

Hulme, W. E. *The Pastoral Care of Families, Its Theology and Practice.* New York: Abingdon Press, 1962.

Johnson, E. S. and Bursk, B. J. "Relationships Between the Elderly and Their Adult Children." *The Gerontologist.* Vol. 17, No. 1, Feb. 1977, pp. 90-96.

Karnes, Liz. *Alternatives to Institutionalization for the Aged: An Overview and Bibliography.* CPL Exchange Bibliography #877. Monticello, Ill.: Council of Planning Librarians, Sept. 1975.

L'Engle, M. *The Summer of Great-grandmother.* New York: Farrar, Strauss and Giroux, 1974.

"Looking to the Z P Generation." *Time.* 28 February 1977, pp. 71, 72.

Maves, P. B. and Cedarleaf, J. L. *Older People and the Church.* New York: Abingdon-Cokesbury Press, 1959.

Murray, John. *Redemption Accomplished and Applied.* Grand Rapids: Eerdmans, 1973.

Nouwen, H.J.M. "Aging and Ministry." *Journal of Pastoral Care.* Vol. 28, 1974, pp. 164-166.

"The Graying of America." *Newsweek.* 28 February 1977, pp. 50-65.

US Department of Health, Education and Welfare. *Rehabilitation and Aging: A Statement of Rehabilitation Needs, Resources and Programs together with Recommendations from the 1961 White House Conference on Aging, Series 11.* Washington, D.C.: Special Staff on Aging, US Department of H.E.W., June 1961.

APPENDIX A:

Conducting a Variety Show

by Becca Weldon, Activity Director,
Crestview Convalescent Home, Wyncote, Pa.

The purpose of a variety show can be twofold: to bring immediate joy and happiness through lively entertainment to nursing home residents, staff and visitors and to create an opportunity for Christians to share their love for God and faith in Christ.

You need only one committed person to start a variety show. His role is to begin things by calling others and persuading them to share their talents for at least one show. You will find that your performers, after their first performance, may be quite eager to make a more long-term (perhaps once-a-month) commitment of their time.

The talent coordinator may also be responsible for contacting the nursing home. He should contact the activities director and set up a show time that's most convenient for all involved. If a piano is required, he should find out whether the home has one available. He should *always* call in the morning of the show and speak to the nurse in charge. She must be prepared for your arrival and be aware of your needs, schedule, etc.

It is not necessary, but it may be useful in some cases, that rehearsals as a whole group occur. Each performer can practice his part alone but he should communicate with the coordinator about his needs for music, time and props. Do leave yourself enough time before the show to pray together and plan the order of the acts.

Find someone with an outgoing personality and a good loud speaking voice to be the Master of Ceremonies. The M.C. is a key figure, especially in adding a "spiritual note" to the show. Perhaps he could work up a short, humorous story with a deeper spiritual meaning. If he tells this at the beginning of the show, it can be referred to at appropriate points throughout the show to reinforce the meaning.

Costuming is important. Bright, flashy colors bring joy and laughter, as does exaggerated makeup. There is no need to spend a lot of money—sew your own (every actor doing his/her own), have a bake sale to raise money or buy from thrift stores.

Older audiences enjoy many kinds of entertainment. Avoid anything that is especially "modern" such as folk-rock guitar and singing. Here are a few suggestions:
1. Old-time sing-along

2. Juggling
3. Banjo/harmonica/accordion/trumpet (in fact, any instrument)
4. Short piano solos
5. Vocal solos
6. Clowns
7. Tap dancing
8. Soft-shoe
9. Skits

A word about recruiting your talent: The acts that you are seeking are not supposed to be professional. In fact, they don't have to be polished performances at all! Their function is to have fun and provide an opportunity, if you desire, to share your faith. For this reason you should encourage interested amateurs to perform. Keep in mind that children, too, can make a very important contribution to your show. Older people truly love to see children. And even if some of the kids are too small to participate, bring them along anyway. But be prepared—they invariably steal the show!

APPENDIX B:

Large-Print Literature

When we first began seriously to visit nursing homes, we knew very little about the availability of large-print literature. As a result, we decided to begin making our own! Even after discovering several sources of large-print material, we decided to continue producing our own materials because we could make them fit certain situations and teach beleifs that we consider important. We have observed that there are three kinds of needs that require special, large-print literature:

1. Special occasions: Birthdays, Christmas, Easter, Good Friday and Valentine's Day are occasions when people are both eager for and accustomed to receiving special greetings. We have found considerable enthusiasm and appreciation for appropriate greeting and special-occasion cards.

2. Themes for meditation: Some of the many themes of the Christian faith and Christian life lend themselves to being treated briefly in a booklet or handout. Such publications could be distributed after a sermon or during a visitation time to encourage meditation. These handouts provide an opportunity for visitors to show that they care about the spiritual needs of those they visit.

3. Prayer: We have been convinced of the great contribution the elderly can make to the kingdom of God as they pray. One focal point of prayer is the world mission of the church. To help direct prayers to that end we have produced many large-print prayer reminders on specific countries of the world and the Christian mission efforts operative in these countries.

If the concern of the literature to be distributed is Christian prayer, we are selective, giving the literature only to Christians (and to those who are especially eager to have a copy). Generally, however, we freely distribute the literature hoping that it will open doors of interest on the part of those who receive it. One must always ask permission before distributing literature in a home and give copies to the staff, if they desire them.

Suggestions on the Production of Large-Print Material

1. Use large, clear printing—it is an absolute necessity.
2. Use familiar images and symbols, for example, the cross or crown of thorns for Good Friday.
3. Keep the message simple and to the point.
4. Leave adequate margins and don't crowd pictures or writing.
5. Be creative. Involve artists in the production.

List of Publishers of Large-Print Materials
(Adapted from a publication of the Library of Congress)

Abingdon Press
201 8th Avenue, South
Nashville, Tennessee 37202

Religious materials, including inspirational titles and prayer books.

American Bible Society
1839 Broadway
New York, New York 10023

New Testament and portions of Scripture in several versions.

American Printing House for the Blind
1839 Frankfort Avenue
Louisville, Kentucky 40206

Christmas songs (words only).

American Scripture Gift Mission, Inc.
1211 Arch Street
Philadelphia, Pennsylvania 19107

Augsburg Publishing House
426 S. Fifth Street
Minneapolis, Minnesota 55415

Religious materials, including devotional items and Bibles.

Back to Bible Broadcasts
Box 82808
Lincoln, Nebraska 68506

Religious books, primarily for older readers.

Baker Book House Company
P.O. Box 6287
Grand Rapids, Michigan 49506

Three religious titles.

The Beavers
Star Route, Box 184
Laporte, Minnesota 56461

Selected Bible verses.

Braille Circulating Library
2700 Stuart Avenue
Richmond, Virginia 23220

Inspirational books and Scripture portions.

Broadman Press
127 Ninth Avenue, North
Nashville, Tennessee 37234

Religious materials, including hymnbooks.

Christian Mission for the Sightless
Rural Route 1
New Ross, Indiana 47968

Spiritual Light—quarterly magazine related to missionary work. (Free)

Christian Record Braille Foundation, Inc.
4444 South 52nd
Lincoln, Nebraska 68516

Bible correspondence courses and other general and religious materials.

Cokesbury Regional Service Center
5th and Grace Streets
Richmond, Virginia 23261

Adult Bible study magazine, based on international lessons.

Concordia Publishing House
3558 South Jefferson Avenue
St. Louis, Missouri 63318

Bible and other religious materials, including a Lutheran hymnal.

Forward Movement Publications
412 Sycamore Street
Cincinnati, Ohio 45202

Forward Day by Day — daily Bible readings and devotions.

Guideposts Associates, Inc. Carmel, New York 10512	*Guideposts:* a practical guide to successful living—magazine.
Logos International 201 Church Street Plainfield, New Jersey 07060	*Prison to Praise*
Lutheran Braille Evangelism Association 660 East Montana Avenue St. Paul, Minnesota 55106	Various religious materials.
Lutheran Braille Workers, Inc. Sight-Saving Division 495 9th Avenue San Francisco, California 94118	Various religious materials, including sermons. Some items available in languages other than English.
John Milton Society for the Blind 29 W. 34th Street, 6th Floor New York, New York 10001	*John Milton Magazine* — digest of religious magazines and devotional articles. (Free)
Thomas Nelson Publishers 405 Seventh Avenue, South Nashville, Tennessee 37203	Giant-print Bibles in several versions.
Fleming H. Revell Company 184 Central Avenue Old Tappan, New Jersey 07675	Religious poetry and devotional materials.
Tyndale Bookshop Mailorder 501 S. Schmale Road Carol Stream, Illinois 60187	Religious materials.
The Upper Room 1908 Grand Avenue Nashville, Tennessee 37202	Devotional materials.
Word Books Division of Word, Inc. 4800 West Waco Drive Waco, Texas 76703	Religious titles.
Xerox Reproduction Center Department XB 200 Madison Avenue New York, New York 10016	Materials enlarged upon request. Other Xerox Reproduction Centers may also provide this service. Send for more information.
Zondervan Publishing House 1415 Lake Drive, S.E. Grand Rapids, Michigan 49506	Several editions of the Bible and other religious books.

Further Information about Large-Type Materials

Church and Synagogue Library
    Association
P.O. Box 1130
Bryn Mawr, Pennsylvania 19010

Provides free book lists and other information about large-type religious materials.

Reference Section
National Library Service for the Blind
    and Physically Handicapped
Library of Congress
Washington, D.C. 20542

"Reading Materials in Large Type" —reference circular listing producers and distributors of large-type material, selected large-type materials, and information concerning services to the visually handicapped. "Volunteers Who Produce Books"—free geographical listing of volunteers who will produce materials not otherwise available in braille, large-type or recorded formats.

Large-Print Greeting Cards

Skilton House
930 Olney Avenue
Philadelphia, Pennsylvania 19141

Those associated with the production of this manual have for many years produced their own greeting cards for use in nursing home ministries. Cards for Christmas, Good Friday and Easter are presently available, with other holidays also being considered. The cost of these cards is minimal.

BIBLIOGRAPHY

(Organized and annotated by Sharon Fish)

General Books on Aging

Hessel, Dieter, ed. *Maggie Kuhn on Aging*. Philadelphia: Westminster Press, 1977.

Gray Panther leader speaks her mind on aging.

Kastenbaum, Robert. *Growing Old: Years of Fulfillment*. New York: Harper and Row, 1979.

Very comprehensive and informative overview of the aging process and needs. The photographs of older people are alone worth the book. Each tells a story about an aspect of growing older.

L 'Engle, Madeleine. *The Summer of Great-grandmother*. New York: Farrar, Straus and Giroux, 1974.

Maclay, Elise. *Green Winter*. New York: Readers Digest Press, 1977.

Free verse poetry written from the perspective of the elderly themselves. Must reading for people visiting nursing homes.

Nouwen, H.J.M. and Walter J. Gaffney. *Aging: The Fulfilment of Life*. Garden City, N. Y.: Image Books, 1976.

Riley, Matilda White et al., eds. *Aging and Society*. 3 vols. New York: Russell Sage Foundation, 1968.

Tournier, Paul. *Learning to Grow Old*. London: SCM Press, 1972.

Personal counsel by a seventy-two-year-old Christian physician on preparation for retirement and what to do when you get there. Author is a beautiful role model of healthy spirituality and the spiritual dimension is integrated throughout.

Biblical Perspectives on Aging

Clements, William M., ed. *Ministry with the Aging*. San Francisco: Harper and Row, 1981.

Series of excellent chapters from various points of view including theology, philosophy, psychology, sociology and medicine. Fine focus on historical/biblical models of aging. Practical helps for congregations make it a practical reference for pastors and lay leaders.

Cook, Thomas C., Jr. and James A. Thorson, eds. *Spiritual Well-Being of the Elderly*. Springfield, Ill.: Charles C. Thomas, 1980.

Thirty chapters by persons from diverse disciplines related to gerontology and theology provide a broad perspective of research and practical application. Main argument is that spiritual well-being is an important element in the quality of life of older adults that has been overlooked and attempts are made to define what spiritual well-being means.

Hilter, Seward, ed. *Toward a Theology of Aging*. New York: Human Sciences Press, 1975.

Essays on the psychological, socio-historical and theological meanings of aging in human life.

Interdenominational Task Force on Aging. *Aging, a Theological Perspective*.

15-page booklet about older persons and the process of aging. Write Presbyterian Senior Services, 2095 Broadway, Room 302, New York, N.Y. 10023 for information.

LeFevre, Carol and Perry LeFevre. *Aging and the Human Spirit*. Chicago: Exploration Press, 1980.

A reader in religion and gerontology. Theory and practical applications.

Stagg, Frank. *The Bible Speaks on Aging*. Nashville: Broadman Press, 1981.

Book-by-book study of the biblical perspective on aging.

Aging Parents

Anderson, Margaret. *Your Aging Parents: When and How to Help.* St. Louis: Concordia, 1979.

One of the most helpful books on understanding the dynamics of parent/child relationships in later years. Must reading for people visiting the elderly.

Gilles, John. *A Guide for Caring for and Coping with Aged Parents.* Nashville: Thomas Nelson, 1981.

Written from the perspective of personal experience with author's father-in-law who suffered a stroke and a mother diagnosed as "senile." Incorporates author's attempts to meet spiritual needs. Eighteen chapters. Other references helpful.

Grollman, Earl and Sharon Grollman. *Caring for Your Aging Parents.* Boston: Beacon Press, 1978.

Father and daughter offer reassurance and hope in the face of complex situations and emotions involved in providing care for elderly parents. Written in free verse, each "poem" is a lesson in a significant aspect of aging and caring.

Otten, Jane and Florence Shelly. *When Your Parents Grow Old: Where to Go, Who to Ask for the Help You Need.* New York: New American Library, Inc., 1976.

How to find help in the community to improve the life of older adults.

Regan, Pauline K., ed. *Aging Parents.* Los Angeles: Andrus Gerontology Center, 1979.

Many statistics but valuable chapters on various aspects of helping parents and understanding feelings of both the elderly parent and the older child.

Schwartz, Arthur N. *Survival Handbook for Children of Aging Parents.* Chicago: Follett Pub. Co., 1977.

Chapters on growing old, senility, retirement, institutionalizaton, death and dying.

Silverstone, Barbara and H. K. Hyman. *You and Your Aging Parents: The Modern Family's Guide to Emotional, Physical and Financial Problems.* New York: Pantheon Books, 1976.

One of the best books available offering guidance to adults in understanding their own responses to aging parents. Leads to other references and resources.

General Ministry to the Aged

Arthur, Julietta. *How to Help Older People.* New York: J. B. Lippincott, 1954.

Fish, Sharon and Judith Allen Shelly. *Spiritual Care: The Nurse's Role.* Downers Grove, Ill.: InterVarsity Press, 1978.

Chapters focus on meeting spiritual needs, using the various resources of self, prayer and Scripture. Written for nurses but valuable for anyone involved in visiting the elderly.

Murphy, Sr. Patricia. *Healing with Time and Love: A Guide for Visiting the Elderly.* Los Angeles: Andrus Gerontology Center, 1979.

One of the most helpful booklets available on guidelines for visiting the elderly at home and in institutions. Individual booklets $2.25; cheaper in quantity orders.

The Church and Christian Outreach to the Aged

Clingan, Donald F. *Aging Persons in the Community of Faith.* Indianapolis: Institute on Religion and Aging, 1975. National Benevolent Association of Service to Congregations, P. O. Box 1986, Indianapolis, Ind.

Guidebook for churches and synagogues on ministry to, with and for the aged. Very practical guidelines and additional references.

Dimmock, Albert E. *Ministry and Older Adults: A Survey Questionnaire for Older Adults to Determine Needs and Resources* (Guidelines for use of the questionnaire). Richmond, Va.: The Center on Aging, Presbyterian School of Christian Education, 1981.

A survey designed to help local churches discover needs and interests of older people in their own congregations. Available from the Office of Aging, General Assembly Mission Board, Atlanta, Ga.

Gray, Robert M. and David O. Moberg. *The Church and the Older Person.* Grand Rapids: Wm. B. Eerdmans Pub. Co., 1977.

Backed by solid research and incorporating numerous studies and interview excerpts, this book includes very practical chapters on what the church can do for older persons and what older persons can do for the church.

Kline, Harvey and Warren Eshbach. *A Future with Hope: Aging Creatively in Christian Community.* Elgin, Ill.: The Brethren Press, 1978.

Survey of the biblical attitude toward aging with a focus on both the church and the family as prime targets for helping persons grow older with hope and respect.

Lutheran Brotherhood. *Life Enrichment for the Elderly.* Minneapolis, 1978.

51-page handbook for congregations developing ministries with and by the elderly. Write Lutheran Brotherhood, 701 2nd Ave. South, Minneapolis, Minn. 55402.

Chapters include: What are our goals? How do we begin? What are our resources?

McClellan, Robert W. *Claiming a Frontier: Ministry and Older People.* Los Angeles: Andrus Gerontology Center, 1977.

Presbyterian minister shares guidelines for congregational ministry by drawing on personal experience at Chatsworth Adult Center, Point Loma Community Presbyterian Church, San Diego, Calif. Good reference for churches seeking role models.

Manual to Assist Congregations in Their Ministry to the Elderly. Philadelphia: Presbytery of Philadelphia, UPUSA, Dept. of Church and Community, 2200 Locust St., 1977.

Manual stressing older people's needs and how congregations can help meet them.

Maves, P. B. and J. L. Cedarleaf. *Older People and the Church.* New York: Abingdon-Cokesbury Press, 1959.

Seltzer, Rabbi Sanford. *So Teach Us to Number Our Days.* New York: Union of American Hebrew Congregations, 1979.

Helpful in understanding needs of elderly people who are Jewish. Practical helps for ministry.

Peterson, James A. and Michael Briley. *Widows and Widowhood: A Creative Approach to Being Alone.* New York: Association Press, 1977.

United Church of Christ minister discusses various stages of grief and processes of adjustment. Most helpful for understanding grieving process.

Shelly, Judith Allen. *Caring in Crisis.* Downers Grove, Ill.: InterVarsity Press, 1979.

Bible studies for helping people with spiritual needs and the use of self, prayer and Scripture in ministering to people as a visitor.

Westberg, Granger. *Good Grief.* Philadelphia: Fortress Press, 1977.

Probably the most helpful book you can read on understanding the grief process and helping someone through it. Also available in large print.

Books Specific to Nursing Home Ministries

Burger, Sarah G. and Martha D 'Erasmo. *Living in a Nursing Home: A Complete Guide for Residents, Their Families, and Friends.* New York: Seabury Press, 1976.

Specifically directed toward nursing home residents and their families but valuable for anyone visiting nursing homes. Talks about choosing and evaluating a nursing home, legal rights of residents, reactions to institutionalization by both residents and families.

Mission Action Group Guide: The Aging. Birmingham, Ala.: Women's Missionary Union, Southern Baptist Convention, 600 N. 20th St., Birmingham, Ala., 1972.

A guide to witnessing and ministering to the elderly.

Peckham, Charles W. and Arline B. Peckham. *Thank You for Shaking My Hand.* Otterbein Home, Lebanon, Ohio 45036, 1977.

A guidebook for volunteers and those who direct them in long-term care facilities.

Other Resources

About Aging: A Catalogue of Films. Los Angeles: Andrus Gerontology Center, 1979.

Aging and the Aged: An Annotated Bibliography and Library Research Guide. Edited by Linna Funk Place, et al. Boulder, Colo.: Westview Press, 1981.

The Ethel Percy Andrus Gerontology Center, University of Southern California, Los Angeles, Calif. 90007. This center is an excellent source of information about films, literature, research, etc.

The National Interfaith Coalition on Aging, P.O. Box 1986, Indianapolis 46206. The NICA publishes a newsletter, sponsors conferences, disseminates research data and acts as a clearinghouse for information and action on the aged.

Peege. 28-minute color film available from the Andrus Gerontology Center (address above). This is "must" viewing for groups visiting nursing homes.